Edinburgh Review 122

Belongin Place

Edinburgh Review

EDITOR: Brian McCabe
ASSISTANT EDITOR & PRODUCTION: Jennie Renton
REVIEWS EDITOR: Michael Lister
WEBSITE DEVELOPMENT: Peter Likarish
ADDITIONAL ASSISTANCE FROM: Hannah Adcock, Fiona Allen, Julia Boll
Catherine McDonald and Ryan Van Winkle

Published by Edinburgh Review
22a Buccleuch Place, Edinburgh EH8 9LN
edinburgh.review@ed.ac.uk
www.edinburghreview.org.uk
ADVISORY BOARD:
Robert Alan Jamieson, Gavin Miller,
Colin Nicholson, Faith Pullin, Randall Stevenson

ISSN 02676672
Edinburgh Review 122 ISBN 978-0-9555745-3-5
© the contributors, 2008
Printed and bound in the UK
by The Cromwell Press Ltd, Trowbridge, Wiltshire

Individual subscriptions (3 issues annually) £17 / $27 / €27
Institutional subscriptions (3 issues annually) £34 / $54 / €54
You can subscribe online at www.edinburghreview.org.uk
or send a cheque to *Edinburgh Review*
22a Buccleuch Place, Edinburgh, EH8 9LN
Back Issues are available at £5.00 each.

Edinburgh Review
is supported by

Edinburgh Review is a partner magazine veurozinew.eurozine.com

Contents

FICTION

Ten things you should know about Australia *Meaghan Delahunt*	13
Chop Chop *John Barker*	46
Bringin the old ones home *Gayle Kennedy*	65
Extract from *Swallow the Air* *Tara June Winch*	98

POETRY

Tom Pow	26
Samuel Wagan Watson	30
James Charlton	35
Les Murray	50
Gordon Meade	51
Martin Harrison	61
Sarah Day	68
Karen Knight	79

ARTICLES

| Belongin Place
Ruby Langford Ginibi | 7 |
| A Submerged Population
Will Brady | 38 |

Poem Country   54
Martin Harrison

Protecting the Great Barrier Reef   72
Pat Hutchings

An Island Home   89
Kim Scott

The Ecology of Australia   102
Mark O'Connor

Extract from *Whispers of this Wik Woman*   133
Fiona Doyle

PHOTOGRAPHS
John Kirk   83

REVIEWS   145

Those rocks are where our clever ones learned to throw their spirits and levitate and talk to the wind and all the elements. They were likened to the great yogis of Tibet with their spiritual powers. They had the power to heal and the power to kill.

Ruby Langford Ginibi

Ruby Langford Ginibi

Belongin Place

In September 1998, at the NSW Writers' Centre in Rozelle, we had the first Indigenous writing workshops. They ran for a week and I was delighted to be asked to attend. There were Aboriginal writers from all over Australia comin. A national conference, it was.

There were two New Zealand teachers, one a pakeha and one Maori, who were the convenors of these workshops. The Maori woman, Eva Toia, gave us all a stone from New Zealand and asked us to write a story about it and a place that was special to us. This stone took my memories back to the old Richmond River at Coraki, where my dad and all his family were born, and where I was born too.

When we were kids we used to go fishin in the Richmond for mullet and garfish. And when the rains came, lookout! The old river would burst its banks. Water laid around for days and days after. Us Koori kids collected pebbles and flat stones and would skim the water as we threw them, makin ripples that grew bigger and bigger with every stone that was thrown.

This mighty river was the lifeblood for the early settlers, the squattocracy, in the late 1800s. Steamers came up-river with produce for the farms along the river banks and the little townships. It emptied into the sea at Ballina, whose tribal name was Bullina, meaning 'blood running from wound', where sharks came upstream, following the schools of mullet when they were spawning.

Cabbage Tree Island mission was about sixteen kilometres from Ballina, and it was home to many of my relatives. My dad's younger sister Phyllis lived there with the Marlowe family after her parents Sam and Mabel Anderson, my grandparents, had died. I remember Aunt Phyllis was not much older than me, though she was a strapping teenager, and she and some of her friends once rounded me up and took me in a boat across to the mainland, rowing up the back channels that watered the plantations and farms. We helped ourselves to bunches of bananas and pumpkins and squashes that were grown. On coming back, I soon found out why they took me with them. The damn boat was so full of this produce we'd nicked that it was just a few centimetres above the waterline. I cried out, 'Auntie, I'm not comin in this boat with you again! There's damn sharks in this water and we might sink! It's a long way to the island if we do!'

I frantically baled the leaky boat with a little bucket. Auntie and the others laughed at me, calling me a scaredy cat while I nearly gunanged myself with fright.

This old river had acres and acres of sugar cane farms. Years ago, big cane punts used to cart the cane that was cut by cane-cutting gangs downstream to the sugar-refining mill. I remember my father had a cane-cutting gang and I'd have to boil the billy for their morning tea. After the cane had been burned to get rid of the snakes, the strong smell of burnt cane was everywhere, the air was full of it. I loved to cut pieces of cane with the big knife and chew the sweet pith of it until I got bellyache!

These are my memories of that special place of mine, the old Richmond River. Now I only have six of my children left out of my family of nine, and my dearest desire is to take them all back home to this Bundjalung country, to connect up with all our mob, our family and extended family, to go to the mission at Coraki, which in our lingo means 'meeting of the waters'. I want to take them and show them all the sacred places. It's my way of handing on our history, our culture and Dreaming. And I won't rest until I've taken them all back so they will know where their roots are, so they in turn will teach their children, and our Dreaming will never be lost, or die out, ever.

*

Some years ago now, in the 1970s, the little village of Nimbin, not far from Bonalbo where I grew up, had an invasion from down south. All the hippie-type people landed looking for spirituality in places like the Rainbow Café. The spirituality these people were looking for was Aboriginal spirituality; Nimbin is a very sacred place to my people, the Bundjalung tribes, because the Nimbin Rocks was the place where our clever men, the *wuyun gali*, were buried. There's a little spirit warrior whose name is Nimbungie who guards the master's teaching place, and he's still there! Those rocks are where our clever ones learned to throw their spirits and levitate and talk to the wind and all the elements. They were likened to the great yogis of Tibet with their spiritual powers. They had the power to heal and the power to kill.

Because the white man often has no respect or regard for our cultural beliefs, teachers have been taking school children on excursions there. The kids have been having bad dreams at night, as this little warrior Nimbungie comes at them in their dreams with a spear to frighten them off. This place is so sacred that our Auntie Milly Boyd, now deceased, was given the job of being carer of this place, even though it's not a women's place and only initiated men could go there. As the old men died off, Aunt Milly had to become the carer so, because it's not a women's place, she'd call out in lingo to the old ones, telling them she was there looking after the place. When she left she'd pick a branch off a tree and brush her footprints off where she'd walked.

White and multicultural people have to learn to respect our sacred sites or their spirits will harm you. Wollumbin (Mount Warning) is another sacred place for men only. Women are not allowed there. The *jurbhihl* or sacred spirit of the place is the gugunguddaba or brush turkey. But now Nimbin is one of the biggest drug places going, not only with ganja but also speed and smack and other prohibited substances too. There's even been a few drug murders there, so the place has some character, aye? So much for spirituality!

I call Bonalbo my 'belongin place' cause it's the friendliest town on the North Coast, the place where I spent the best years of my life. Me and my two sisters had a happy childhood there, even though we were the products of a broken home. I remember old Grandfather Breckinridge, our elder. Old Ted's father had a big brigalow bush growing at the back of his house in Coraki. He used to have these little bantam chooks who had their nests in little baskets and round dishes he had fitted into the forked branches of the tree so the eggs wouldn't fall and break. When us curious little black kids wanted to know why they laid only tiny little eggs, grandfather would chuckle as he told us that they were rooster's eggs. Us kids were too silly to realise that roosters never laid eggs at all. No wonder grandfather was chuckling, aye?

I remember the guavas growing all round the common, and lots of locuts, a yellow fruit with big seeds in it. Also the big old fig tree right at the gate to the common, near the dipping yards, where they dipped the cattle and horses for ticks. This was the common we had to go across. It was a shortcut to the town, which was so small it could be called a village. This little place had only one main street, right on the banks of the old Richmond River, which was the lifeblood of the small townships on its banks: Lismore, Casino, Ballina, Wardell, Broadwater, Woodburn, just to name a few.

We attended the little bush school in Bonalbo. There were about fifty of us kids, with classes running off the big verandah. The farm kids used to ride their horses to school, and let them feed around the schoolyard. They'd take the bridle and saddle off then saddle them up to ride them home after school.

We all had our jobs to do before school in the morning. I was the cowgirl and we had about four or five house cows to milk. I had to get up early each morning and milk them, hand separate the milk and put the cream in a big bowl in the ice box and keep it until Saturday, when I'd chuck a handful of salt into it, get the big wooden spoon and make home-made butter. After the milking was done, I'd turn the cows out of the yard to feed all day, then round them up in the afternoon. It was dark by the time I milked them again and I rugged them up in wintertime. If male calves were born to the cows when they were calving, the men of the family would have to doctor them up, castrate them, making them into steers, so we could fatten them up to sell at the cattle sales each month. While they were doing this, us kids would be hidden away and the calves would be bellowing like buggery.

Me and my two sisters slept in a big double bed. I was the eldest at eight years old and had to sleep in the middle. The little ones were so frightened of the dark. Gwennie would be in the back with her legs chucked over me, and Rita the baby was in front of me with her arms around my neck too. Mother Nell would check us out at night and disentangle their arms so I could breathe. She thought they might choke me.

At night we'd have to all go to the toilet before bed. There was no electricity then and it was a long way outside. We would roll up a long piece of newspaper, light it with matches to see our way to the loo, then stand with our legs crossed, nearly piddling ourselves while we shooed the frogs out with the lighted paper. When I became a woman many years later and lived out in the scrub doing bush work like burning-off or fencing, I had to kill snakes to protect my kids. But to this day I still won't go near a frog!

We attended Sunday School, and at Xmas time the minister would round up all us kids and we'd go around the township, ringing bells and singing Xmas carols.

We had concerts in the old picture theatre where Gwennie and me used to sing 'To you sweetheart, aloha, from the bottom of my heart', with these big hula grass skirts on to dance in.

We were involved in everything – there were no exclusions in this town, no prejudice, no nothing. Weekends, a gang of us kids would go up Gorge Creek looking for wild fruit and bush lemons, geebungs and wild cherries. Mother Nell used to make pies out of the cherries, she was a deadly cook with the old fuel stove. And Father Sam, he'd be palming the cakes that she'd made out to us kids. She'd be asking, 'Father, where's all those cakes I made gone?' and he'd say, 'I don't know, Mother, the fairies must have took em.' Us kids would run, leaving him to take the blame.

Evenings we all would sit in the front yard in summertime and Father Sam would bring a watermelon out. He'd cut it up and rub the skin into our faces and through his beard. The old radio, which ran on batteries, would be playing Jack Spearing's dance band on a Thursday night. Mother Nell loved listening to it.

I am saddened every time I have been back to Bonalbo over the last few years. This town I call my real belongin place is going downhill. The only pub got burned down. They replaced it with a portable in the backyard and carried on regardless, selling the grog, but there's no place for all the stockmen on cattle sale days. There is only one small bed and breakfast place.

I first went home to Bonalbo in 1986 for a school reunion. Me, and my two sisters, and Mother Nell's other daughter Shirley. It was not the town I remembered. The butter factory stood idle and lonely on the banks of

Peacock Creek, with only memories of the beautiful full-cream Norco butter it used to make. The Greyhound coaches went a long time ago, along with the big timber mill. There were two shops and one bank. There used to be two garages – now I think there's only one, situated on the Woodenbong Road, that sells newspapers and petrol and oil. There was Stewart's Bakery a long time ago, but not now, and a hospital on the hill. The school was huge now, going up to fifth form, and there was a swimming pool, a bowling club and a camping area.

We went to our old street, where our old house used to be. But there was not a thing left of the old house. Just all the memories we shared. We walked away sadly. I wish with all my heart that I could turn back the hands of time and make Buna-walbu come alive again like it used to be. But alas, all I have is my lovely memories of my real belongin place.

Bonalbo derives its name from the Gidabal word meaning 'bloodwood trees'.

'Belongin Place' is an extract from *All My Mob* (University of Queensland Press, 2007).

Meaghan Delahunt

Ten things you should know about Australia

We spoke on the phone at least twice a week. A long-distance call. We were close like that.

'You're writing about here?' My twin sister's voice always went up at the end, even if it wasn't a question. It pitched even higher when she was excited. 'You're coming back?'

'No.' I'd made up my mind. 'I'm not coming back.'

I'd lived in Scotland for twenty years and rarely set foot on my native soil. In general I avoided writing about Australia. Too many bridges crossed. Too many exes. Not to mention my mother.

'Then how can you write about it?' I could hear she was disappointed. 'You're not going to call it Oz are you?'

'Of course not.'

'Or Down Under?'

'Promise. But you'll have to help me.'

'I'll try.' She sounded hurt and was trying to push it down. Our family specialty.

'I need an idiot's guide to Australia,' I said. 'For an in-flight magazine. Ten facts.'

'Depends,' she said. She was stalling. Making me work. 'What Australia are we talking? It's a big multicultural joint.'

She was making it complicated.

'Whatever happened to White Australia?'

'He's in power. He plays cricket. He mouths off. The world has heard enough about Him.'

'OK,' I said. My twin was a Linguistics Professor. Gender was her thing. She thought my travel writing glib and Bryson-lite although she never said this to my face. She was always trying to edge my work towards the deep. Back in the day, I'd fancied myself as a lyricist in the Chatwin mode. Or fashioned myself after Sebald – all back-weighted German sentences, all that melancholy. In truth, though, I was an entertainer. I knew this about myself. I didn't like to disappoint. I was a clown. I preferred laughter to tears. There was nothing deep or complex about my work, the words came easy and I liked it that way.

'Let's narrow it down,' I suggested. 'Melbourne – third largest Greek city in the world…'

'Is it still?' My sister was unsure. 'You need to get your facts straight.'

'That's why I called you.'

'OK,' she sighed. 'I'll check it out.'

'After Athens and Thessaloniki,' I went on. 'Any Greek will tell you.'

'OK. Fine.' she said. 'Ten things you should know?'

'Yep.'

'*Numero Uno*: Asylum seekers. We lock 'em up, we throw away the key. Separate them from their kids. Build internment centres in the desert. Watch while they go on hunger strike, sewing their mouths shut with bits of wire…'

'I don't think…'

But my sister was on a roll. 'How about this: Our myths are all rural but our reality is urban?'

I sighed. 'Look, really. No one wants this kind of stuff…'

'Then there's the drought. A farmer tops himself every four minutes…'

'Look,' I said again. 'You know that won't wash. It's a bloody in-flight magazine.'

'Or this…' I knew she was winding me up. 'Aboriginal Australians… why can't we say sorry?'

'Who do you think I am?' I said. 'The *Guardian* bloody newspaper?

'Jesus! Give me something good. Nothing political or disturbing.'

'That's very Australian,' she said, with a smile in her voice. 'To preface a remark with "Look".'

'OK, Professor.' I knew she'd forgiven me for not coming back. 'Give me something I can actually use.'

'Right,' my sister said. 'I get your drift. You want the simple stuff. But not too simple. You don't want to sound like Bryson do you? Please say you won't go for the easy laughs. Please don't mention the term "Down Under".'

At the mere mention of Bryson, my sphincter tightened. 'No way.'

'You want the stuff that reinforces what the reader already believes. You want to know the latest lingo and the non-threatening ways of White suburbia at the barbie?'

'Exactly.'

'In short, the same old shit.'

'It's how I've made my name.'

'You could write something good one day.' She disapproved of light entertainment.

'But would it pay the bills?'

'Well,' I could hear her reluctance. She wanted to lecture me (yet again) on wasting my God-given talents. What she didn't realise was that I was actually playing to my strengths. I made a good living, got to travel the world. Meet some pretty women. I was a natural-born coward and happiest in my comfort zone. Why shake things up now?

'Let's start with the abbreviations,' she said. 'Any word of two syllables,' she paused, 'even a word of one syllable, can never survive in this country. Everything is abbreviated. Everything. Afternoon becomes "arvo", breakfast becomes "brekkie", sandwich becomes "sanger".'

'Got it.' I scribbled it all down. 'A glossary.'

'If you came back once in a while,' her voice was suddenly full of reproach, 'you'd remember these things.'

I pretended not to hear. 'What else?' I was writing long-hand and holding the phone under my chin. 'How about the flora and fauna? Brits love flora and fauna.'

'I thought it was pets.'

'They think it extends to all animals.'

'OK. We've got it all sewn up. Everyone knows. The Great Whites offshore; the killer sharks in Sydney harbour. The marauding jellyfish and the Bluebottles. We've got killer crocs and fresh-water crocs that also kill.' She tapped the phone. 'Only now they tell us. About the fresh water… And we thought they were friendly…'

'With those teeth? Go on.' [← 'come on']

'What about the snakes? The Tiger snakes. The King Browns. The Pythons. Not to mention the Taipan. Then there's the spiders. Funnelwebs in Sydney. Red Backs in Melbourne. God only knows what else. Then the blow-flies, the mosquitoes, the ticks and the leeches. The sand flies…'

As she said all this I had a flash-back. A trip to North Queensland many years ago. My leg full of purple bites that became ulcers. Up North, the air hummed and buzzed and everything was always eating everything else. I still had scars from those bloody sand-flies. Jesus, I thought, you'd be mad to visit some of these places. Grown men dodging jellyfish, swimming in stocking suits, bottles of vinegar on shore as antidote. Who knew what could get you? It all came flooding back: Australia was a crawling, heaving, nightmare of dog-eat-dog. Dog-eat-baby, if we counted the dingoes.

My ex mother-in-law had once kept a special supplement on Australia from the *Scotsman*. It was a map of all the dangerous animals, insects and plants. Where to go. What to avoid. She never went. She avoided completely. She despised all things Australian. This became acute after I separated from my Scottish wife of fifteen years. I'd like to report that my ex and I remained best of friends and that I didn't put her mother off all Australians for life, but I'd be lying.

'Something's always out to get you,' my sister said happily, interrupting my thoughts as if she'd read them, which maybe she had. 'All the development now – up north and in the west. It's boom-time on account of China. Selling uranium and iron ore like there's no tomorrow. Like a new gold rush. Even the locals are out to get you…'

'Have we covered things that bite?' I asked, a little impatient.

'I think so. We should move on to survival. Over here it's all about survival.'

'It is?' I'd forgotten about survival. I'd lived too long in a place with no sun, no mosquitoes, no flies, no killer jellyfish or venomous snakes, no hole in the ozone. I'd forgotten what survival meant.

'All the way to Sydney. Signs everywhere. It's all about water, sunscreen, bushfires, fruit fly, the works…'

'Fruit fly,' I muttered. How could I have forgotten? All those childhood road trips interstate, our parents smoking all the way with the windows up, choking us in the backseat. Me and my sister munching through bags of grapes and oranges, apples and bananas, making ourselves sick the closer we got to the border, munching as if our lives depended on it. Men in blue uniforms and caps giving the car the once-over – a stray apple core could be your undoing. Australia was strict like that.

At every border, they were on the ball. They never let up.

The airport was the worst. On my last trip, the sniffer dog at Tullamarine had nailed a pack of Bombay Mix – half-open – completely forgotten in my hand luggage. I'd been grilled at customs for an hour.

I realised that there was a thesis here that could never be developed in an article for an in-flight magazine. There was obviously something about contamination and contagion, some rampant virus in the White Australian psyche worth exploring, I thought. The need to contain a perceived menace with penal settlements, or refugee camps, fruit fly inspections and sniffer dogs at airports. It occurred to me that the War on Terror had been part of the mind-set for years. I wondered if the Qantas stewards still sprayed unsuspecting passengers – to fumigate them, to deodorise them – to what, exactly? It had always been a mystery. Just when you were at your most vulnerable before touch down, two stewards would stalk the aisles, aerosol cans in hand, no warning, and spray right through you.

There was something deeply unsettling about it all. But because I wasn't a Chatwin or a Sebald I'd never see this thesis through. I knew that my shallows had hidden depths but I had to stay focused or I'd never finish this damn article.

I'd brooded over two hundred years of White settlement in thirty seconds and brought myself back to what my sister was saying. I'd zoned out because my twin was now talking about our mother. 'She just doesn't know how to be kind to me,' she said. I could hear the familiar despair in her voice.

This was so true, and I'd heard it so often, I was always lost for words. I'd been born ten minutes ahead of my twin and this seemed to have made all the difference. My mother never took to my sister, simple as that. I was the good twin and my sister was the evil one. I'd spent my life defending her from our mother's strange and unpredictable onslaughts.

It was my sister's favourite topic and I was a little weary of it, to be honest, but I indulged her out of a sense of Catholic guilt. Knowing I was the favourite child. Knowing that my mother felt upset at my divorce. Knowing that she'd never bonded with my twin. All I knew was that my mother loved me so much I'd felt compelled to put continents between us. Meanwhile, my sister, always dutiful, stayed close, put in an appearance every week and got dog's abuse. My sister had always longed for affection and sought it in a series of disastrous men who treated her exactly like our mother. Unfortunately, she'd married the last bloke and had a child with him. The kid was very sweet, but the last time I'd seen him he was five. Soon he would be fifteen.

My sister shifted her attention from our mother to her soon-to-be-ex-husband. She was going through what could only be described as 'an acrimonious divorce'. Did divorce come in any other form? I was curious, having just been through the process myself. Love turned into its opposite so quickly. The minute the game was over it was as if there had never been any game, any play, any good times at all.

'How's it going?' I sighed to myself, wondering how I would ever get off the topic of her divorce and onto my article.

'Think of two suicide bombers in a market place,' my sister said. 'Both detonating at the same time.' She paused. ' That's how bad.'

'How's Stevie taking it?' Stevie was my little nephew.

'He seems fine. One week on. One week off. Every second weekend with his father. It's been nine months. He's getting used to it.'

'You must miss him.'

'I hate his guts.'

'I meant Stevie.'

'Of course. I miss him. But it's also good, to have the space. To think about my life, y'know? Like, if I don't feel like eating, I don't have to…'

My sister had a fraught relationship with food. She'd been a plump child and our twig-thin mother had taken it as a personal affront. Packed my sister off to WeightWatchers at the age of twelve. On the few occasions we'd spent together as adults, on holiday, say, or when I was back in Australia, my sister would push food around her plate at meal times but in the early hours of the night I'd hear a strange rustling in the kitchen, and the fridge door slide open and shut, and in the morning I'd notice certain items gone – a litre of milk, a half a pound of butter, a packet of cheese, all the leftovers. I never confronted her about it. I mainly worried.

More to the point, I worried about the effect this weird eating behaviour would have on young Stevie. I hoped he hadn't inherited the worst of both parents – his mother's eating disorder and his father's everything else.

His father worked for the Foreign Office. I'd always suspected that he worked for ASIO, the Australian Secret Service, under cover of the Foreign Office. Anyway, his father, my brother-in-law, was a pain in the arse. Every conversation was a battleground. It was bloody exhausting. You'd say something off-the-cuff like, 'There's a child born every three seconds.' Mr Foreign Office would snort, 'More like 2.5.' He was always contradicting, always competing, and it got on my goat.

My sister was going on about Mr Foreign Office. I interrupted. 'Enough about you. What about me? I'm working to a deadline here.'

She laughed. 'OK. OK. I'll give you a whole list: Always swim between the flags. Don't go out in the mid-day sun. Never run from a house during a bushfire. If a shark attacks, punch it on the nose. If a wave dumps you, keep rolling. If you get caught in a rip swim with it… any Australian knows this stuff.' She took a deep breath. 'And finally – put everything in the fridge.'

I'd never questioned the wisdom of this last point until my ex-wife drew attention to it. On our first trip to Australia together we'd stayed in the family home. She'd complained constantly (to me) about the 'O'Casey bread.' She'd almost lost a tooth, she said, biting into a slice. 'Your mother's bread is frozen,' she said. 'And if it's not cold, it's damp.' My mother kept everything in the fridge. To defrost, she'd put everything in the microwave for ten seconds. I don't know whether I could generalise from this to all Australians but I did notice that the majority put most items on ice. Butter and bread. Honey and Vegemite. Tomatoes, mushrooms, bananas; the works. Everything went in the fridge and came out like it'd been to the Antarctic.

'Any more advice?'

'Sunscreen and a hat,' she said. 'And always reapply. The only people with tans are tourists…'

Just for the hell of it, I thought I should generalise about the national character. I made the mistake of saying this to my sister.

'Friendly? Open? Big smiles? You live here for long enough and you realise we're the same pack of selfish bastards you see everywhere – only we're more laid-back about it.'

'And mateship?'

'A colonial myth. Blokes in the bush. Women-folk in the kitchen. If Germaine didn't exist, we would've had to invent her.'

'Is that all?'

'That's about it. Nothing political or disturbing, right?'

I'd almost finished my article way ahead of schedule, but all this talk of Australia was getting to me. It was mid-winter in Edinburgh and we'd hardly had a summer. It was my first Christmas since the divorce and I guess I was feeling lonely. More than that, I was starting to think I'd made a big mistake. The woman I'd been seeing had stopped returning my calls. I'd left my marriage for her and now I was wondering why. Then my sister got on the blower and said I ought to come for a visit. Ten years was too long, she insisted. I hadn't been back since our father's funeral. Mum hadn't been herself lately, and it would soon be Stevie's birthday. And so I did something I'd sworn off doing for another decade: I booked a ticket to Australia. I booked Emirates because of the leg room and the 500 channels and the decent in-flight food. Even if the other airline was paying for my article, on a long-haul they were always crap. Any Australian could tell you.

It was true what they say. Jet lag got worse as you got older. The Melatonin tablets made no difference. When I finally came to consciousness, I'd been in Melbourne almost a week. I'd noticed that everything was big and sunny, and that was just the people. I'd been eating and drinking like a king (very cheaply) and then sleeping and waking at odd hours. I'd been forced to repeat whole phrases in restaurants and supermarkets on account of my accent. My speech patterns were all over the shop. In Scotland they knew I was Australian, but over here, in cafes and bars, on the trams, they just thought I was some Pom with weird 'r' sounds. I felt as if my head were being shaken up and rearranged. As the days wore on though, my speech started morphing into something else altogether. I was starting to sound more Australian than all the Australians around me. More specifically, I was starting to sound like a bloke from the 1950's. I was starting to sound like my father. It had to be more than the jet lag. I was even starting to think in old-time Australian words and phrases. 'Have a go, ya mug,' I wanted to shout at the Prime Minister doing his election spiel on television. 'Streuth,' I found myself saying. 'Crikey.'

At the end of that first week, feeling just about human, I came down to breakfast in my sister's house at a reasonable hour. My nephew, who'd been on school camp for a few days and then at his father's, was sitting at the table eating damp toast with marmalade. I hadn't seen him since he met me at the airport. I gave him a big hug.

'So,' Stevie said, patting me on the back. 'You divorced Aunty Jean, right?'

I couldn't believe it. 'Good morning to you too.' I said. 'Teabags?'

'In the fridge.' The kid sounded indignant. 'You gave mum the idea…'

'What are you on about?' I said.

'She left Dad.'

'She wasn't happy.'

'Is it because you're twins?'

'It's because your father was an arsehole,' I said. I couldn't help myself.

'Aunty Jean was great,' he shot back. 'You're the asshole.' He said it in an American accent. The kid had been a lot sweeter at age five, that's for sure. He sat there, full of hostility, his teeth sinking right through the toast, right through the half-melted butter. He finished his toast in silence and started spooning frozen yoghurt straight from the tub. He ate four tubs of full-fat yoghurt a day, my sister said.

'Mate,' I said, surprising myself, because I never call anybody mate, 'don't take it out on me.'

This seemed to calm the kid down. Or maybe it was a calcium-rush. 'You say "yo-gaht", don't you? Like the Queen,' he said, licking the spoon. 'Emphasis on "yo",' he said. 'But Australians say "yow-gert".'

The kid was obviously an amateur linguist, following in his mother's footsteps. A little bit of a pedant, after his father. 'I guess.' I felt confused, all of a sudden. How the hell did I pronounce anything? But I saw an opportunity to break through the bad vibe. 'Hey. I want to run some words past you.'

Stevie looked suspicious and indifferent all at once. The way only a teenager could look. 'OK.'

'How about "dag"? Do kids still say, "What a dag!" or "How daggy!" or, "You look like a dag?"'

My nephew looked blank. 'Dag?'

'As in stupid or unattractive or, if said affectionately, to mean: "What a character!"'

21

'Um.' He raised his eyebrows. 'No.'

'How about,' I persevered. 'How about – "drongo, shonky, galah?"'

He shook his head at me and rolled his eyes as if I'd spoken Mandarin.

'How about, if something is really great you say, "It's grouse!"'

'No.'

'"She'll be right mate?"'

'No.'

'"G'day?"'

'Only if you're old. Or on *Neighbours*. We don't say any of that shit.' My nephew snorted, exactly like his father. 'We say *cool*, and *dude* and *doh* and *way to go*.'

'You speak like an American.'

'Everyone speaks like that. It's. Like. Cool.'

Stevie sounded vaguely American, now I knew why. It was deliberate. I felt a moment of sadness that all the old words were vanishing. Had all Australian kids become high school sophomores trawling malls, looking for prom dates?

'How about "To wag school? To go for a root?"'

'Je–sus,' said my nephew, in his quasi-American voice. 'A root? That's having sex, right?'

'Yep.'

'That's disgusting.'

Then he leant back in his chair and went a little green around the gills. He'd munched his way through half a loaf of damp toast and two cartons of full-fat yoghurt. He gripped his stomach and then gladdened my heart by using an old expression that even I'd forgotten.

'Uncle Ro,' he said, 'I'm feeling pretty crook.'

I stayed in Melbourne for a month and saw my mother twice. On my first visit she said, 'Your sister's put on weight.' We avoided all talk of my failed marriage and my ex-wife, who she'd never been keen on. She scrutinised my outfit. 'That shirt's a little loud,' she said. 'You must be doing well for yourself.'

Occasionally she would mention her grandson, Stevie, but without any enthusiasm. 'He has his mother's figure,' she sniffed.

'He's a good kid,' I countered. He was driving me up the wall, but I didn't want to give her any ammo.

'He could be.'

She didn't have a good word to say about anything. Not even about the election result, which I thought would've pleased her.

'At least the Liberals are out,' I said.

'It's a country of drongos,' she shook her head. 'Idiots.'

On my second and last visit, the day was hot and humid and I noticed she was a little breathless.

'It's that bad north wind,' she said to me gasping a little. 'You know that wind?'

'I think so.'

I knew that what she really meant was: 'Do you even remember what it's like here? Why did you go so far away?'

'The hot wind,' she repeated.

'Uh-huh.' I remembered the wind, but I'd always been lousy with direction.

'Anyway,' she coughed. It was a dry, high cough that seemed to afflict her on days like this. Something I did remember from childhood. 'I knew I had something to tell you. The Cutter's house. Behind us. You remember?' She gestured out of the kitchen window. 'Well, it's gone. Bulldozed. Two days it took. And I feel upset, Ro… every time I look out.'

I followed her gaze and it was only now that I could see the level space behind the trees at the back fence.

'They left those damn trees,' she said. 'Who knows why?'

'Bastards,' I said. Which seemed to please her.

'One day it took. Then the next day they got a bulldozer. And I felt… I felt really sad. Y'know? Developers bought it. From W.A.' She'd always despised the neighbours and I thought she would've been glad to see the back of them. My sister was right. She obviously wasn't herself.

She paused and I could see she was trying not to cry. My mother was always on the verge of tears but never giving in. Since we were kids she'd been like that. It'd always been my job to distract her from herself. Make her happy. Only now, for some reason, I didn't feel up to the task.

She sat with her hands in her lap. She looked down at her hands twisted with arthritis. Then she looked up. 'I felt life was finished,' she said and her voice cracked a little. She shrugged, trying to be light-hearted. But we both knew that she was never light-hearted. There was always something sticky and heavy and unsaid underneath. She frightened me now because she was so direct. I was used to oblique and jagged conversations on the phone, waiting to cut myself on a stray comment, usually about my sister. My mother seemed suddenly very pale and old.

'You better go and have a glass of water. A lie-down,' I said to her, trying to soothe. 'It's hot. Maybe you're dehydrated.'

'Well, your Uncle Den had a turn yesterday.'

There'd been a dinner at my uncle's house that I'd managed to miss.

'A turn?'

'On account of the heat. He was fine one minute. Next thing you know, he keeled over.'

'Fainted?'

'Who knows? It was embarrassing. But what do they expect?' Her voice suddenly went hard and angry at the seams, her familiar voice. 'What they don't realise is. They're all old. All of them over seventy. Why stand on a hot day? They should be sitting down…'

'Well…'

'No one saw me standing.' She seemed very proud of the fact.

My mother would soon be eighty. Somehow, she always managed to blame the victim. Next thing she started up about some cousin's wife who had tickets on herself, but what she really meant was the cousin's husband. She was sounding confused. She looked chalk-white. I was glad that she was sitting down.

'Mum, I think you need to…'

'I'm feeling a bit…' she conceded.

'I'll just get you some water. Lie down.' I surprised myself by sounding authoritative.

She lay down. I got a face washer and put it in cold water and placed it on her forehead and held her hand while she stretched out on the couch and this was the first time I could ever remember looking after her in any way. And it was a strange sensation, for both of us.

'Are you really leaving tomorrow?' she said. 'So soon?'

I didn't answer, but I held her hand and made soothing noises and watched unfathomable tears slip down her cheeks, under her glasses, and soon she was asleep and I sat there a long time watching her. There was a framed photo of my father on the mantelpiece that I tried to avoid.

I let go her hand and moved to the sink to get some water for myself. Through the window I could see the blank space behind the fir trees and the beginnings of what looked like a block of flats. I was conscious that if I'd been a different kind of writer I could maybe have explored all this in a different way. All these changes. But I was an entertainer, for God's sake. *I was a fricking sad clown.* I stood at the sink, compiling every fact I'd ever known about Australia into a definitive list. Wanting to finish that damn article. Weighing up everything I'd ever thought about the place. The words came heavy. I could feel hot ugly tears building at the back of me but I fought them off as I got my mobile from my pocket and walked out into the backyard.

The day was blue and close and the north wind bore down. A cockatoo screeched high through the fir trees and right into the marrow of me as I dialled my sister's number and waited for a signal, impatient to make contact, wanting to get through.

Tom Pow

From *A Wild Adventure – Fragments from the Life of Thomas Watling, Dumfries Convict Artist*

Transported for forging bank notes in 1792, Thomas Watling (b. 1762–d.?) was the first professional artist in Botany Bay. His paintings (most of which are held in the Natural History Museum in London) form one of the principal records of the earliest days in Australia. The Lord Advocate noted that as, 'an ingenious artist, [Watling] will be an acquisition to the new colony at Botany Bay'. Seconded to Surgeon-General John White, an amateur naturalist, he was made to work hard drawing the flora and fauna of the settlement, though on the back of one of his drawings, White felt compelled to write: 'The pride and vanity of the draughtsman has induced him to put his name to all the drawings, but should you publish them I think the name may be left out.' Watling was pardoned in 1797 and was back in Dumfries by 1803. In 1805 he was arrested for forging five guinea notes, but the jury found the case not proven.

Three poems from *Thomas Watling*

It's a small attic room and there's light –
the good light he needs – from a lamp

on the table before him. His eyesight's
not what it was. At times his hand cramps

when he needs it to be steady, as he steers
his pen round the double-cupped curve

that begins *Bank*. Sometimes, he'll squeeze a tear
of concentration; through it catch the swerve

of a bird, its plumage smudged in shadows.
He gave them all the pictures they asked for –

the Channel Bill, the Needle-tailed Swallow –
but he should've attended to their calls.

Then the common cries of pigeon and crow
couldn't confuse him. There wouldn't be a note

or a song that, from this cold room, could draw
him back to a world that was carved from light.

In the candlelight he looks at his hands –
two maps; two different destinations.

Call one hand Innocence. Slowly it turns
from darkness into light and he catches

in it something of a human presence
that is shocking and fresh, like the raised bands

of flesh that decorate their naked chests
or the cloth-like folds of an old buttock.

Though the left won't knowingly do you harm,
the right has had a different schooling.

Callused, where the fingers like a socket
hold the brush, his lifeline's planted with grains

of ink down each tiny tributary.
The right has no scruples: what it sees, it paints.

The left closes on itself like a shell:
he doesn't really know it at all.

The screams are like crystals in the cold air;
each one of the same kind, yet each unique

in the way it trails or anticipates patterns
of pain. Some *zek* is getting his Dozen.

After the first strokes, his back is streaked
with blood. The rhymes that follow will tear

the flesh away. 'That'll teach the Oirish!'
some fool shouts. The rest look to their work.

The earth is frozen; it will yield nothing.
The cold-eyed birds and the glassy-eyed fish,

and all the other creatures that lurk
in this place, know it'll soon be over.

There are times Watling must break the ice
to get at his paints. Some time when he does

he'll catch a forgetfulness that covers
this land; its bone-white Siberian cries.

Samuel Wagan Watson

I'd rather call myself a 'Guerilla' wordsmith than an 'Australian' writer. What I present to an audience could be classed as textual postcards; visions through Indigenous retinas of consciousness, picked up upon my journey. My writing doesn't comply to the common formats of how English literature should be presented, but, how much English literature has actually protected my culture and lands? In this country, Indigenous language, voices and writing are still heavily censored or kept down by mainstream media and audiences... Guerilla literature is my tactic, my vehicle, my weapon...

Haibun Cowboy

I've been riding this white, barren country for weeks it seems, and this page, this page for the moment is my country! It is the Invaders' paper in my grasp, but still, it is so inaccessible to many of my kin. I have rustled the Invaders' dictionary, driving an entire body of words onto this plain. Circles and circles forged, rotating the herd of nouns and verbs, separating the adjectives in calf and steering the good fat headwords to the northern corral of the border. It was a lifeless piece of paper anyway, and soon phrases will settle, sentences will graze. On the horizon, no clouds of inspiration, but moths have been circling like wedge-tail eagles in the bright hue of the reading lamp, heat bearing down on the paper, winged predators hungrily eyeing off a few straying letters. Sundogs appear on the mind's eye of my sweating brow, whirly hazes dance in the trail of the live-stocks' inky smears. Please, let it rain…This page for the moment though is my land, extinguished of title and void of ghosts.

Cannot write for days,
Temperature rising fast,
The drought lingering…

Monster

I can't speak my grandmother's tongue and I've never been on my grandfather's land. I've traveled here and I've traveled there, my culture fabricated in government-funded laboratories…I am Frankenstein of the Dreamtime, I am Frankenstein of the Dreamtime. Reanimated flesh that once sung natural song-lines, surgically removed my Christian soul and repaired it with Indigenous design… I am a patriot to a black, yellow and red flag, yet I am colour-blind… I am Frankenstein of the Dreamtime. I am a mutation of the white Australia policy, I am Frankenstein of the Dreamtime… I am in John Howard's nightmares, I am an educated Aborigine, I am John Howard's worst nightmare, I am Frankenstein of the Dreamtime… I scare some white people with my English, I am a Frankenstein of the Dreamtime. Today people will sing, Advance Australia Fair, and like the abomination that I am, I can only ask Advance Australia Where? Thinking black is a thought-crime, I have no need for Queen or desecrated country, only Australian nationalism can define, I'm a renegade of Indigenous context, I am Frankenstein of the Dreamtime…

Parallel Oz

It's the Lucky Country's closet; a dark interior with frontier skeletons. Whirly-winds run rampant, spawning red-sand mandalas of chaos. These frenetic twisters find easy prey on ochre-kissed Dorothys, carrying them off to Parallel Oz. In Parallel Oz, neither the Good witches or the wicked afford these Dorothys' little pairs of magic red shoes… there's no place like a broken home… there's no place like a broken home… there's no place like a broken home. The yellow-brick road is pockmarked with massacre sites and the Wizard, the Wizard of Parallel Oz; he holds Dorothy hostage to a mutual obligation agreement. The Straw-man has the grazing monopoly, the Tinman has the mines, and the Lion waits in the spinifex, with the long-grass drinkers. Parallel Oz and it's rag-doll Dorothys; not just an Advance Australia Fairytale, but a reality spinning out of control, gaining catastrophic momentum…

Welcome to No Man's Land

All the signs read, SMILE... YOU'RE ON CAMERA, Welcome to No Man's Land, you're standing on Terra Firma, that some explorer once coined Terra Australis, and another explorer then retouched with Terra Nullius, that stole this land's dreams, Terra Firma could be the next target in the War on Terror, from Terra Australis, to Anti-terror Laws, SMILE... YOU'RE ON CAMERA, Welcome to No Man's Land, Terra Australis, with its Terra Firma, deemed Terra Nullius, embroiled into the War on Terror and everyone is governed by Anti-terror Laws, SMILE... YOU'RE ON CAMERA, Welcome to No Man's Land, population under observation, you gotta love a sun-burnt country with a dry, split personality, Terra Australis, under Terra Nullius, right where you're standing on Terra Firma with its beauty and its Terror, Terror, Terror... Welcome to No Man's Land.

James Charlton

Mangrove Swamp

Mudskippers splatter their bodies
onto mud banks,
                flash dorsal fins,
breathe from water-filled gill chambers.

Pairs of fiddler crabs bolt into holes.
Males wave their claws;
the females have caught on.

From mud, root shoots protrude
like nails, serve as stilts,
or thrust in and out.

At night, bats,
contorted as burnt match boxes,
frot mangrove pollen to set seeds.

Stroked by parental shadows,
young plants snorkel in brine.
Silt becomes mud
becomes land…

the whole swamp veined like a womb,
heaving and sighing;
heaving with a sucking sound
and a sigh.

To Governor George Arthur in Heaven

You didn't fornicate, swear or drink.
You didn't cheat or hate.
Each night, studying Scripture,
you thanked the Lord for dying to save you.
In the mornings you dangled the guilty.
Their throats were tightened after prayers,
and *all but the most insensible*
showed signs of repentance.

I should not judge –
you did not choose your code.
But talk with Mary MacLauchlan,
dragged from husband and family in Glasgow;
transported for theft to Van Diemen's Land.

Remember stretching her for infanticide,
8 a.m., Monday, April the 19th, 1830?
At least you couldn't sleep –
struggled with that verse about yea be yea
and nay nay – and shunned the leading citizen
who seduced her.

Ask Mary about that final letter
to two small daughters,
and life's last walk, on air.

Note: Lieutenant Governor of Van Diemen's Land from 1823 to 1837, Arthur was under New South Wales jurisdiction and answerable to the Home Office at Westminster. Lines 17 and 18 reflect the version of Matthew 5:37 with which Arthur was familiar.

Yellow-tailed Black Cockatoos

Random as rags whooshed off a truck,
    they indolently amble on the air. This caterwaul:
        wee-la. Yes, there,

husky, high. It seems an idle sortie,
    a lope of meander-flight, a frittering in the eye
        of foul weather.

Gale winds begin to split and peel
    a suburb of weather-board husks, but the flock
        keeps following its memory-grid

to grubs in weakened trees. (Birds like these
    saw dinosaurs plod through dust.)
        They prise, rip,

rasher the acacia bark, and change trees,
    wheeling and veering like black Venetian blinds
        collapsed at one end.

Then they dip, curious,
    to an English willow;
        shimmy down bare verticals on hinge-claws;

whir out
    on a glissade of whoops:
        concertina-tailed, splay-winged, wailing.

Will Brady

A Submerged Population

Four middle-aged men embark on a weekend fishing trip. They drive into the mountains, park the car and hike several miles to where they want to fish. The first evening at the river, even before they have set up camp, they discover the corpse of a young woman, naked, floating face down in the water. They talk about what they should do and decide, rather than abandoning the trip, to delay reporting the body. Having tethered it to the shore, they spend the following day fishing, alerting the police only on their return.

This is the premise for a short story by American writer Raymond Carver. More accurately, it is the pretext; the girl, it transpires, was raped and murdered, but the story is concerned not so much with this tragedy as its aftermath. Grounded as always in the banal, Carver is interested not in the death itself (for which he offers no explanation), but how differing responses to an event of such magnitude can expose the emotional tensions that lurk just beneath the surface of everyday experience. Thus the story opens not with an account of the murder but with Stuart, who found the body, returning home, hungry and tired, sitting down to dinner. His wife, Claire, having learned what has happened, is horrified at her husband's casual indifference, while he himself is unwilling, or unable, to recognise its profundity. 'Something has come between us,' Claire confesses to the reader, 'though he would like me to believe otherwise.'

'So Much Water So Close to Home', first published in 1977, is typical of Carver's fiction: a study in what he termed 'dis-ease' – disillusionment and miscommunication in the lives of ordinary people. As usual, events are played out in this quotidian context; it is here, when the veneer of domestic harmony disintegrates, that we glimpse the malevolence beneath the mundane.

Chekhov once said that there are two 'poles' to a story: 'him' and 'her'. Carver's stories are often charged with a tension which owes much to the polarised attitudes of men and women, particularly as they manifest in moments of crisis. Here, in essence, we have a moral quandary: what are the obligations of the living to the dead? Carver suggests that men and women approach this issue very differently and that the rift that opens between Stuart and Claire functions as a microcosm of the gender division that exists in every marriage.

Carver's world is immediately recognisable as proletarian America. His stories, almost without exception, are set in the American Midwest – though seldom in a *specific* time or place. Pervaded by a mood of timelessness, placelessness, isolation from politics and historical events, they seem to be happening both nowhere and everywhere. Carver himself confirmed a proclivity for the generic; his essentialist view of human nature urges us to read the American location of his stories as ultimately irrelevant. The contours of his world are defined not so much physically as psychologically; we are invited to enter not a place, but a predicament. This predicament, Carver would have us believe, is one of universal relevance.

This goes some way to explaining why, though by no means a household name, Carver has been translated into over twenty-five languages and his stories the subject of numerous adaptations for stage and screen. In 1993, Robert Altman included 'So Much Water So Close to Home' in his patchwork homage *Short Cuts*, seamlessly transplanting Carver's characters to a Los Angeles suburb. The filmmaker Ray Lawrence recently undertook a more daring upheaval, translating the story to his native Australia.

The town of Jindabyne lies in the foothills of the Snowy Mountains, New South Wales. In the 1960s, it was intentionally flooded by the damming of a river. The original settlement, left at the bottom of a newly created lake, was rebuilt nearby and is today a skiing and fishing resort. The town's 'drowned' history becomes an uncomfortable metaphor in Lawrence's film: the implication of a submerged population provides an apt basis for addressing Carver's themes of displacement and denial.

Jindabyne tries to remain faithful to the ethical core of the story on which it is based, while necessarily embellishing Carver's frugal narrative. The strained relationship between Stuart and Claire continues to be of central concern here, though as we soon learn, theirs is not the only struggle – the other men and their partners must wrestle with skeletons in their respective closets also, while the community at large is forced to address some truths long suppressed.

Lawrence and his scriptwriter, Beatrix Christian, have endeavoured to make *Jindabyne* not only a film about male insensitivity and female empathy, but also an exploration of what these sexual politics might tell us about Australia's current social climate. Until at least an hour into the film, we can read the men's behaviour in fairly straightforward terms – further evidence, should any be required, of man's capacity for inhumanity to man – or indeed, to woman. A feminist reading of the film would surely not overlook the brutal subjection of the murdered girl and would presumably speculate – as Claire does – that the men might have acted differently had the body they found been that of a boy. Before drawing any conclusions in this respect, however, we are forced to consider an even thornier question. The incident inevitably becomes a scandal in the hands of the local media and in a TV interview, the murdered girl's family asks: 'Would it have been different if she had been white?'

Here the film departs from Carver's essentialist symposium on gender politics and attempts to address a problem of specific relevance to contemporary Australia. The dead girl is Aboriginal and her family's assertion that the men's neglect was racially motivated prompts condemnation from the Aboriginal community, who are quick to make accusations of 'white hate crimes.' While never this explicit, we must now consider the possibility that the men's indifference is not ethnically indiscriminate. So *Jindabyne* becomes, somewhat belatedly, a film about racism – or rather, a film about the latent racism embedded in contemporary Australian culture.

Since the earliest years of European settlement, Australia's white immigrant, migrant and indigenous groups have been embroiled in fierce debate about 'rights to belong.' As sociologist David Mercer has observed, the heady days of colonial vigour which followed the publication of Adam Smith's *Wealth of*

Nations made the 'new' Australia 'a kind of living laboratory for liberalism... where Social Darwinist ideas of white superiority... gave legitimacy to a raft of exclusionary and even eugenic policies.' And while the Commonwealth's 1948 Nationality and Citizenship Act made it clear that all who were born in Australia – regardless of colour – were legally citizens, this piece of legislation proved to be an empty vessel; the evidence overwhelmingly suggests that Australia's Aboriginals and Torres Strait Islanders still remain largely 'citizens without rights'.

The question of citizenship has in recent years been the subject of growing public debate in liberal democratic societies. According to Mercer, this debate ought to be framed in the context of three core ideas that have gained widespread acceptance. First, that 'the notion of citizenship has been debased and diluted from its original ideal of active participation to mere formal and passive membership'. Second, 'the significance of past historical wrongs against particular ethnic or indigenous groups invariably is glossed over and the assumption is made that enlightened educational campaigns are all that are required to make redress'. And third, 'there is the view that liberal democracies are now genuinely 'multicultural'; people of all races, colours and creeds are treated equally and welcomed as citizens'. These ideas are seriously open to question, particularly in the context of Australia.

Today, Australia occupies an awkward liminal position, belonging neither to its Anglo-centred past nor an assuredly post-colonial future. The centenary of the Australian Constitution was marked in 2001 and with the recent election of a new Government, it is certainly timely to reflect on the changes that took place in the twentieth century – and to consider those ahead as we settle into the twenty-first.

The mainstream white views of Australia's indigenous population have gradually shifted from complete indifference or active promotion of genocide, through assimilationism – a transparently racialist project with the clear aim of eliminating 'minority' cultures through a continual process of absorption – to the current position of grudging recognition and 'reconciliation'. Even the terminology is misleading. It implies that at some stage in the past the Aboriginal and non-Aboriginal people had a relationship which operated on mutually beneficial terms, that this relationship has deteriorated and that reconciliation is now a plausible (or even desirable) solution. A policy which in theory looks unrealistic at best, in reality has proved deeply insidious:

former Prime Minister John Howard's penchant for 'practical reconciliation' often translated into savage cuts to many Commonwealth government programmes designed specifically to assist indigenous people. Earlier this year, a radically interventionist plan to tackle alcoholism and domestic violence in Australia's most disadvantaged communities was denounced as racist by, among others, the Aboriginal Medical Services Alliance. The measures – including compulsory medical checks and bans on alcohol and pornography – and the motive – so nakedly a strategy to win votes in the run-up to an election – are in themselves questionable. More troubling, however, is institutionalised discrimination, which exacerbates the social malaise endemic in Aboriginal communities.

This discrimination operates in subtle ways. As Mercer notes:

> 70% of Aboriginal households in Western Australia are forced to live in rental accommodation and all but 8% of these rent their homes from the State public housing agency, Homeswest. In the 1990s the conservative State government's agenda was to reduce State debt and one strategy was to escalate the eviction rate for bad debtors. Inevitably, the resultant institutional discrimination took a heavy toll on indigenous people. One estimate was that in 1998 around 60% of the evictions involved Aboriginal families even though less than 20% of public housing units in that State were taken up by indigenous people.

Aboriginal and Torres Strait Islanders, who together make up about 2.5 per cent of Australia's population, live on average seventeen years less than their fellow citizens. The average life expectancy for Aboriginal men is fifty-nine, compared with seventy-seven for non-indigenous males, according to a 2006 report by the Australian Institute of Health and Welfare. Australia has the dubious distinction of being the only first world country with a dispossessed indigenous minority whose men, on average, will not live long enough to claim a retirement pension. Suicide rates among Aboriginals are between three and four times that of their non-indigenous counterparts. The educational level is much lower than the national average, the imprisonment rate as much as sixteen times higher. If, as Dostoyevsky suggested, the degree of civilisation in a society can be judged by entering the prisons, this statistic alone raises serious questions about the legitimacy of the Australian state and the extent to which it has continually failed its Aboriginal citizens.

The fundamental problem turns out to be the *ir*reconcilability of two cultural ideologies. The principles of Australia's liberal democracy give precedence to the rights of the individual over those of the group. In addition, with its emphasis on economic liberty, the liberal democratic state has considerable difficulty dealing with spiritual values that are so central to Aboriginal being.

Australia today remains a deeply conservative country. The latent desire to remain a white liberal state, unchallenged by ethnic minority discontent is evidenced by increasingly stringent control of its indigenous population. There is a perception that escalating flows of immigrants threaten to compromise the very idea of territory as a sovereign space over whose borders an *authorised* public has the sole right of movement, ownership and voice. Anderson and Turner, in 'Exclusionary Politics and the Question of National Belonging', write:

> Anxieties reached a peak in late 2001 around the 'Tampa affair', when the conservative Howard government intercepted and denied 433 rescued asylum seekers entry into Australia and precipitated an international controversy... [T]his moment at which Howard drew 'a line in the sea' to keep asylum seekers out, was one of moral crisis for Australia. 'Border protection' became the catch-cry that justified an immediate series of official exclusionary practices.
>
> (*Ethnicities* vol. 5 no. 4)

The perception of an *external* threat, in the form of immigrant invasion, can be linked with an *internalised* settler-society anxiety embedded within the problematic colonial origins of the Australian nation and the thwarted cultural codes of its indigenous population. The latter's dispossession, argue Anderson and Turner, 'casts a shadow over the unproblematic heroic narratives of 'white settlement' and continues to haunt the discourses of a benign and united sovereign nation.' An apology for past injustices to indigenous Australians remained an 'unsayable' act for John Howard for the duration of his tenure. As a symbolic disavowal of the country's 'black history,' Howard's stance suggests 'a kind of historical defensiveness that is analogous with defending the assumed-to-be-white space of the nation.'

In short, racism in Australia seems to be tied to the spatial dimension of its settlement project, where an antipodean sense of place manifests as 'spatial anxiety'. In *Jindabyne*, we can read the behaviour of the men as representative of the latent racism in contemporary Australia – racism founded on an attitude of indifference and manifest now in a crisis of belonging. Significantly, the character of Stuart, in Lawrence's reworking, is attributed an Irish heritage, which seems to be a deliberate attempt on the part of the director to approach the problem of settler anxiety. The fishing trip, which has become an annual ritual in the lives of these men, stands for a primal urge to reconnect with the land. Discovering the girl's body is, in a sense, a violation of this impulse; while their subsequent behaviour cannot be excused, it can, in this light, be better understood.

Likewise, Claire's reaction can be seen as symptomatic of the same anxiety, albeit surfacing not in moody denial but a post-colonial guilt complex. She too is an immigrant and, as a reviewer in the *New York Times* puts it, 'stereotypically American' in her handling of the trauma, 'pushing toward the therapeutic goals of healing and closure, while her white Australian friends urge her to move on and let go of her fury and shame'. Enraged by the complacency of Jindabyne's predominantly white population, she embarks on an ill-advised fund-raising campaign, seeking to make some reparation to the Aborigine community, only to be rewarded with hostility from both.

Stuart's unwillingness to accept responsibility for his actions and Claire's clumsy efforts toward tolerance and respect, are, in essence, two stages in the same process. *Jindabyne*'s proposal – that racism has not yet been eradicated from white post-colonial societies, that it lurks, submerged, within a population's consciousness – is an important idea, explored here with intelligence and tact. It is, for the most part, an intricate and well conceived film, though, as A.O. Scott points out, 'too many of the incidents, sub-plots and conversations have been stuffed into the delicate vessel of Carver's story, rather than allowed to grow organically out of it.' Carver is a master of ellipsis; often his stories resonate not with what is said, but what is left unsaid. Something of this has apparently been lost in the translation from page to screen (or from short story to feature-length film): *Jindabyne* seems at times disconcertingly like a soap opera. Arguably however, the film's greatest flaw comes in its denouement, which features an Aboriginal smoking ceremony and an unlikely convergence of oppositions that the rest of the film has carefully teased apart. Here, men and women, whites and Aborigines, the sacred and the secular, even the living and dead, are reconciled, momentarily at least, in what approximates a happy ending. This reconciliation feels contrived and unconvincing, an injustice to the enquiry initiated by the film.

While we could scarcely expect *Jindabyne* to offer a solution to Australia's problem of latent racism, we might have hoped, as we hope now of Australia's newly elected government, for emphasis not on 'reconciliation' and 'consensus', but more realistic goals of accommodation and compromise.

John Barker

Chop Chop

He must press on. No time to be lost. If there ever had been time to lose, he did not remember it. Sunday evenings? Perhaps, evenings when he should be sat down with his dreams but even then, how could anyone cross their heart and say that was lost time. How could you win without having your dreams?

This Sunday evening he could only remember his dreams. He must press on. A small misunderstanding when night was falling and the girls must be fresh for the dawn because Mr Brown too, he was pressing on. Expansion, a new contract, was what he'd said, and the agency must supply, or he would have to look elsewhere. It was nothing personal, he said, the big Englishman in his suit and his smell, the pressed white shirt undone at the collar, but that was the situation, all must be just in time.

He must press on, pushing the girls like the donkeys they were, stupid girls from the north, from villages on stony ground. Hurry hurry. It was he who must say it, see how was the traffic and say Go! Pulling the handle of the fold-up shopping trolley and the mattress tied on with the octopus grip, pulling the girls at either end. And still the mattress swayed on the trolley as if the girls were not there at all. Till they reached the white line in the middle of the road, after the half-gap had come, the big red bus that had had the time to brake. And there, the sound of the brakes with the white line reached, when it was clear there was only one thing to be done, that the mattress must turn and hold itself along the white line till the next gap came, it was he, sweat on the forehead in the cool night air, him who must make it so. It took all his strength to pull them into the line, the girls, and the mattress that was red with a white zig zag, so as to face the opposite pavement. It was their next objective, the opposite pavement.

It was nothing personal, Mr Brown said, but the consumer is king. Or queen, he said, with a laugh and a slap on the shoulders. And he had said in return, No Problem Misser Brown, because it was no problem till the dice fell bad and there was a small misunderstanding over the room. He'd explained, tried to explain. These stupid country girls, they say they eat only their own food they make themselves. Read the contract pal, Mr White said, No cooking on premises. A rude man. Now they must press on. And these girls, what did they care when everything was laid on for them. Knowing there would always be a bed and some food because someone else would arrange it.

The half-width of road ahead rumbled under the weight of the truck, TESCO lettered along its side. The girls, what did they care. England, where nothing bad happened. Hurry hurry, pulling them through the next gap before the BMW. Pulling because they stared at the car, black, 5 series, like paradise had come to this earth. He would have done it all by himself if the mattress, the double, didn't bend and spring itself like the fattest, baddest serpent. He would have brought the girls separate. One by one or two by two, he'd have brought them, but when there were mattresses also, what could he do? What could any man do?

Till they reached the promised land, him dragging the trolley when its left wheel had tilted on the camber. There, on the other side, a man stared at them. Too bad, there was no time to entertain. Stare what you like. Whereas he, he must press on: the girls must be fresh for dawn, Mr Brown says that's how they must be. It is nothing personal he says, it is contractual quotas.

Over the weekend problems had come his way like a pack of dogs in a village of mud. Scavengers with yellow teeth.

Was a mistake Misser White, he'd said. Poor country girls, they are ignorant.

It was not his problem, Mister White had replied. Contractual obligations had not been met and they must go.

On the pavement the girls stood. He must pull the trolley round, them and the mattress with it. They must press on. Of course they must press on. Along the one block, past the *All Night Food and Wine* where no one gave them not a stare nor a glance. This was London Town. There was enough entertainment already.

A very hard man, Mr White, and then today, the clutch on the Transit had gone. More money from his own pocket and not ready till Monday.

It was not his problem, Mr Brown said, but just this once – and he was serious, just this very once -- he would arrange transport for the pick-up. 5.30 a.m. sharp, and the girls must be fresh, fresher than fresh salads, he'd said, and laughed at his own joke.

The address?

He'd said he would ring Mr Brown later with the address, waiting for a joke at his expense or worse, Mr Brown saying enough was enough.

And now, he must take the next risk, leaving the girls on the corner with the mattress while he checked the new place was safe, no sign of the bandit landlord himself or any neighbour busy fellows.

He told them, stay there, and don't talk to no one. Everywhere in the world there were bad men and in London too, he told them. And then there were the police. Any sign of them, they should walk away and leave the mattress. And then return to the corner when everything was OK again. He would be waiting for them. They moved their heads as if they understood, and what could he do but hope even these village girls had done understood. They surely knew what meant police.

And he must press on. Around the corner he went, his chest tight, the breathing heavy, and unclipped the new keys from his belt. He knocked the door five times before opening up. It's what he'd told them, the first batch: so they would know it was him, told them five times that he would knock five times.

There were four of them with the one double mattress, along with the single bed that came with the room. The light bulb in the ceiling had a pink shade that was stuck in a tilt. A studio flat, the thief of a landlord said, a kitchenette and bathroom squeezed in. But what could he do?! Pay, he had no choice; the girls must be fresh for their work.

No, they said like they were Siamese and all joined at the head, no one else had come round. On his way out he locked the door. Anxious juices were in his belly as he turned the corner, but there they were, with the mattress, just as he had left them. Donkeys waiting to be told what to do next. A couple in crazy coloured clothes were staring at them from across the street. Lucky people with time to lose. They could stare as much as they like, for now they must press on, round the corner with them and the mattress in tow.

Six of them in place now, chattering away their nonsense, not a care in the world. Everything was on his plate. Six more girls, one more mattress and one hour to go before midnight and Mr White round with his friends who would not be friendly friends. He must press on. He folded the trolley flat and told them not to speak to any one, not open the door to anyone, and hurried out. No time for even one cigarette, when this should be his own time, to sit down with his dreams.

Les Murray

Two Scapes

Green-edged terra cotta
mosaics that centre on sport.
Green terra cotta mosaic
labelled with brands and speeds.
Terra cotta housing to the green
and yellow rims of the ocean.
Over all this, the stars
swimming in the night blue
keep their abundant pattern
but an artery or vein,
scarlet, edged with white,
joins finely to each star,
blood vessels converging
high, pulsing downward and up.

Cattle-hoof Hardpan

Trees from modern times don't
bear
but the old China pear
still standing in the soil
of 1880 rains fruit.

Gordon Meade

The Breakwater

Even when it is surrounded,
it still maintains the illusion of being

what it is; and even when the sea
washes over it, it still proclaims, like Canute,
that it can stop the waves. At low tide,

we can see that there has been a hole punched
through it, and on either side of that, two hairline fractures
have appeared. From that, we cannot tell

for how many years it will remain
intact; only that its days are numbered.

The Boulder

There is the face
of a man, and the body
of a woman. There is

the wing of a raven,
and a sleeping seal. And each
one is contained, as if

under lock and key,
within this boulder; this boulder
that every day is dried

and washed, dried
and washed, by the wind
and the sea. Sometimes,

the woman's hair is
green and, sometimes, brown;
and the wings of the raven

will never lift into flight.
The eyes of the sleeping seal will
never open; and the man

must always keep his
mouth and his nostrils firmly shut
just in case he should drown.

The Sea Within

On some days, I almost forget
that it exists; days when it is calm and grey,
and merges with the sky.

                At other times,

it is everything. I can think
of nothing else as it leaps and writhes, moon-
driven and wind-whipped.

                But mostly,

it is just a presence, like a dog
stretched out on the rug; something to remind me
of the animal, both outside

                and within.

Martin Harrison

Poem Country

An essay called 'Self, Place, Newness' collected in my book of essays, *Who Wants to Create Australia?* attempted to make the case for what seems to me to be a strongly emphasised aspect of modern Australian poetry: the attentiveness in the work of many poets to landscape, to the environment and to issues connected with environment. What the essay reflects is the fact that many Australian poets have an exploratory, even a metaphysical and certainly a celebratory approach to country. To look at things in their locales is not just a matter of repetition: there is a genuine aesthetic newness in doing so, and a conceptual challenge. The names of things are not fixed, the celebration of country is intense, often dreamlike, and often problematic in terms of unrecognised histories or previously ill-defined senses of the natural world. The environment may be engaged with subliminally or consciously, but in both cases issues of environmental fragility and destruction are no less unavoidable elements of poetic realisation than is the recognition of the familiar and the beautiful. In fact, writing landscape may be less to do with writing nature than to do with writing and re-shaping a carefully protected Australian myth, a myth deeply cultivated by a nation whose everyday life is mostly urban and suburban rather than rural. I focused this essay around individual poems by several modern, mostly seventies and eighties poets (though not all of them were living). The list was Robert Gray, Philip Hodgins, Antigone Kefala, Peter Porter and Jennifer Rankin. And I was aware that two of these poets, Porter and Kefala, are not normally associated with landscape and that at best only two of those poets – Peter Porter and Robert Gray – have any extensive readership outside of Australia.

Of course, this mix of celebration and tentativeness in relation to the environment is only one trait – no matter how clearly it can be tracked through the work of numerous poets. The seventies and eighties had been a period of debate, divergence and argument in Australian poetry, accompanied by a sudden awareness of experimental and innovative tendencies in American poetry and other foreign poetry as well as by a re-reading of symbolist and modernist French poems. If I think of recent work from poets of that period who continue to write and publish, then the experimental and expert technical range of one of the key figures, John Tranter, comes to mind. Tranter has gone on to produce a large body of work. His poems are often irreverent, parodic, delightfully humorous, and at the same time full of readings and borrowings from a whole range of literary and non-literary languages, whether *haibun* or *film noir*, Hölderlin or airport bookshop doorstopper. Perhaps ultimately his poetry is a constant attempt to return to, and define, a feature clearly evidenced at the start in his writing, particularly in his early cinema-influenced poems. For Tranter's is a poetry whose creative moment both rejoices in and undermines a deep responsiveness to the multimedia and electronic nature of contemporary language. The poems are skilfully eclectic in terms of source texts and of referenced genres, but also in terms of an allusiveness which is at once that of a true littérateur on the one side and an ironic pop cultural tourist on the other.

Is the Australian response to pop culture similar to how popular cultural influences are reacted to anywhere else in the world? Certainly I think popular and film culture has exerted a greater influence on a generation or two of Australian poets than is the case in the UK. It interests me, for example, that such a question cannot help but be asked as soon as the last few decades of our poetry is thought about. What also seems to distinguish the Australian view is a self-consciousness about the imported nature of so much which we enjoy. Popular culture is a guilty pleasure as well as an exhilarating one. This mix of unease and enjoyment carries through into a broader response to language – namely that poetry gathers a multiplicity of languages, a many-sided and often contradictory assemblage of cultural influences, and that the proliferation of images and media which bombard 'our' local Australian space has to be attended to. A few years ago, for instance, I was lucky enough to include two of Jennifer Maiden's poems in a Californian anthology, *Poetry International*. 'Missing Elvis 1' and 'Missing Elvis 2' capture this mix of thrill, eclecticism and unease which marks a communal sense of popular culture images. (The poems were collected later in her 2005 volume *Friendly Fire: New Poems*.) They are meditations on the deaths of John Lennon and of Elvis Presley, but the core image is of the water-bombing helicopter brought in from the USA to fight out-of-control bushfires which struck New South Wales through Christmas 2001. With the brilliance of boyo slang, the helicopter was nicknamed 'Elvis', first by local firefighters and then by local TV stations:

> On his way to deep water
> 'Elvis' the sky-crane helicopter,
> looking like a monster
> from Aliens, flies over
> drops spit-spots on the verandah,
> hovers to talk, as I look up…

I suspect Jennifer Maiden intends and understands every nuance, every gesture, of this moment. In the book *Friendly Fire*, these Elvis poems are contextualised by poems to do with spending nights watching a TV deluged with news items to do with the Iraq War and George W. Bush.

Some of my recent reading includes Laurie Duggan's *The Passenger* which, in a spacious journal-keeping way and swerving between prose and poems, reflects this same mix of dissonances and thrills in an everydayness filled with consumer objects, news and celebrity. Or I have been looking at Michael Farrell's cut up, recombined *War Poems* which sample mainly the work of First World War poets, and some of which appear in a new book next year. Or I have been looking at the highly improvisational jazz-influenced work of Jill Jones.

Such comments only give a fleeting sense of one part of a creative context and of the variousness of compositional elements. Influences over the language with which we write come from many places, whether geographical, regional, familial, literary, or to do with media and multimedia. Poets discover – I think, however, never with complete freedom – what that place is for them and their work, and what relationship they can or must have with the many contemporary versions of mainstream language and utterance. Sam Wagan Watson has been recently talking about a renegade or outsider position in language. Comments sometimes similar to this are made about another Aboriginal poet, Lionel Fogarty. Responding in a different way to the state of mainstream discourse, the construction of a de-referenced but at the same time highly lyrical language figures in the work of a non-Aboriginal poet such as Peter Minter.

By far and away one of the strongest presences in Australian poetry over the last few decades is Les Murray's. By sometime in the eighties Murray had established a kind of 're-design' of the basic language of modern Australian poetry, drawing on his extraordinary skills as a maker of metaphors but drawing equally on the wide inheritance of literary and subliterary idioms and registers already present in our poetic history. In a talk originally broadcast in 1986 and collected in *A Working Forest,* Murray refers to the danger of losing what he termed a 'colloquial middle-voiced poetry'. Typically, Murray sourced this voice to a genre both ancient and subliterary: the wealth of magazine and newspaper poetry published in nineteenth century Australia. This is a voice which, as he puts it, 'catches a great deal of ordinary human experience and shares it in an unfussed way with a broad range of people.' The whole essay is a fascinating way of talking about the presence and influence of the many sub-poetries whose authenticity and whose naivety can be drawn on in writing poems. Murray is referencing a communal source for poetry, one which mixed up the work of both named and unnamed poets. Adapting a phrase in a review written by the British poet Hugo Williams, he goes on to talk about how this 'middle-voiced' voice links with the capacity of Australian poetry to achieve a 'relaxed modernity' long before the rise of literary modernism, whether in Australia or elsewhere. One implication of the existence of this middle-voiced colloquialism which is neither pre-modern nor post-modern is that Australia has had and still has, a different modernism from other parts of the English speaking world. As Williams put it, it has a 'plausible' alternative modernity to the literary modernism of American and British poetry.

A constituent of this 'middle-voiced' talk has been, in Murray's case, an unabashed willingness to re-invoke bush poetry, popular humoresque poetry of the early twentieth century and the Australian literary form of the bush ballad. Murray is in fact a syncretist of the multiplicity of Australian voices, no less than his work reflects a wide understanding of late modernist English language poetry way beyond Australian contexts. I sometimes think of the first part of Murray's work (up to some date in the mid eighties) as an attempt to create a mainstream 'creolised' form of Australian idiom mainly intended for Australians and the later writing to be an ambitious and courageous attempt to bring the wider range of Australian Englishes into the heartland of the modern and post-modernist landscape of English language poetry everywhere. Whatever the case, Murray's positioning of the vernacular at the centre of his poetry (with its grand parallel with Dante's decision to write in vernacular rather in Latin) typifies the intensity of the question of register and voice in his poetry. Murray himself speaks of 'an unceasing colloquial assembly' in his poem 'The Broad-Bean Sermon' and it could well be applied to his own poetry. In this context, the British critic Steven Matthews perceptively identifies this aspect of his poetry when he speaks of the 'excitement and the sense of risk and affront within Murray's version of an idealised, polydialectical poetic voice, one that speaks for international and republican conditions in the twenty-first century.'

But this brings one back to that question of broader contemporary influences from non- and sub-literary forms – from cinema, from the world of consumerism and celebrity, from mass media and advertising – all of which bring their own idioms. However different, both Murray and the poets of the seventies and eighties share an enlivening, decompressing interest in forms which are sub-literary, slangy and colloquial, even if the source points are quite distinct. Murray's are from the historical and the print community, from the bush traditions, from the world of living and local memory and, largely, from pre-televisual oral traditions. Many of the later generation's poets turned instead to the contemporary lexicon of mass media and popular culture, no less oral and performative than traditional genres are, accepting a language which involves a mix of local and hyper-real references (all those flying cinematic Elvises) which burgeon in global and supra-national image worlds.

All this said, however, poets write poetry as their own act of invention, borrowing, taking and refining. The cross-talk within the surrounding language is nothing in itself, other than material for the clarification and delineation of significant poetry. In this regard, Robert Adamson's recent, prize-winning *The Goldfinches of Baghdad* offers another slant on risk and centrality. A deftly interwoven collection, the poems sometimes directly, but often with a highly indirect subtlety, refer to the current war in Iraq. The undertow of this theme is less overt than in Jennifer Maiden's work. But more than any pre-occupation of this newsworthy sort, these poems reveal how Adamson is also a central maker of Australian language, especially in the fable-based poems to do with native birds. Birds, fish, rivers and the night have been lifelong themes of Adamson's. These recent bird poems ally a sharp-eyed attentiveness to nature and to natural phenomena with something not normally associated with the environment, namely a series of registers way beyond the celebratory, and including satire and the grotesque and parody. A complex set of overlapping types of poetic discourse converge on the ornithological model. At times, they are like John Gould prints, re-sized, re-coloured and collaged with conflicting text and other images. At other times, they are perfect miniatures, in the mode of fine-hair painting and watercolour. At times they are didactic and political like Skelton or Chaucer. At other times, they are direct, transparent and lyrical. Like the avocets of the poem of that title, 'Red-Necked Avocet', these are shape-shifting poems: levels of meaning undergo deep transformation just as the birds who, once seen and captured in experience:

> ...migrated from our
> thoughts into our words and went
> skidding with sound as they
> too became human.

These poems emerge from an intimate poetry close on the ear, but one which skids with sounds in a fertile interplay of vernacular, literary, scientific and classical motifs. There is an openness to accident and experiment in such work. And more than any of his 1970s contemporaries, Adamson brings the multifarious world of poetry back into alignment with the long-lived themes of attachment, traditional memory and Australian environment.

The horizon is defined, or looks defined, only from where you are standing. Besides it is hard to communicate a sense of vision within that horizon if many of the constituents – the things in the middle distance – are unfamiliar or unknown beyond the place you are standing in. That is what the experimentalism and also the risk of finding new names for things brings with it. It may also be one reason why contemporary Australian poetry so often expresses both attachment to local places and, parallel to that, a *need for* – and even a distrust of – such attachment. To a degree, a reading of recent Australian poetry, say, from the late seventies, should be an ideal place for a post-modernist to wander in, much more so than a similar period of writing from the USA or Britain. The difficulty with such a comment is that the play of eclecticism and attachment, of high and low registers, of imported and authentic, has never not been a feature of Australian poetry. Nor is there any single point in our poetic history at which the breaking wave of modernism might be said to have crumbled into a choppy, baroque foam of post-modernity. Similarly, the prevalent and overarching critical view that somehow Australian poetry is a negative tradition – namely, that it operates as a tradition without a poetico-philosophical founder such as a Whitman or a Shakespeare – is belied by the fact that the term 'tradition' takes on very different meanings as soon as the achievements of the last century or so are put in the context of Australian indigenous poetics. You cannot live here and write here, and not have some version of that thought. Whatever the response, including the response of deliberate inattentiveness, a key disposition will be introduced into the poem.

Placed there as an afterthought to do with these issues – though nothing in poetry is really just afterthought – such responsiveness is the particular brilliance of a recent poem of Mark Tredinnick's which I have just read. Classically titled, his *Eclogues* gets right a necessary mix of nonchalance and self-awareness – that Australian contemporary ease – especially in the way it ends. A long poem, it explores equally the local domain of family life and an at once international and local sense of ecological crisis. It has just been published as the first choice of the Newcastle Poetry Prize this year. I read it as one of the judges on the panel. The many-levelled care of the poem moved me, as did the skill with which it blends public and private voices. But so did the tact (and the modernity and traditionalism) by which Tredinnick comes to treat the whole of his poem as a kind of country – a process-oriented environment of spirit and action – in which the future's mind remains unchangeable: the poem, he writes, 'isn't *for* anything: a poem is country,/ and it needs you to keep walking in it.'

Martin Harrison

Drover

Made in America, the old harmonica
travelled the world
once it had taken on in Germany –
it was 'the waist-coat pocket orchestra.'

Electric cars pioneered green Oregon,
with a torque faster than petrol.
Quickly the truth went to Mobile –
it could have gone anywhere back then.

So who counts the millions who now flee
from the firestorm there in the desert?
Only poetry's beyond forgiveness. –
Who dares speak for the dead today?

Tunes shift meaning with an eye's twinkle.
Himmler's daughter thought he was a hero,
spent her life trying to clear his name. A drover,
playing his harmonica, calms the night's cattle.

Dead Grass

It's raining –

in a way, it's raining in the night,
but this night's not the real night
with a belt of rain splayed across it
but the kind of darkness
you feel in separation
from someone you really love
someone you can't see for months

This rain –
whose real version hasn't happened –
slants through the night
which is your mind's darkness
the always unthought part of thought
the space back of the eyes
through the ear's untraced edge

dry invisible rain in the night
sparks of rain like fire
spatters of rain like wind-blown embers
heavier rain – after a lightning strike – pouring like fringes of lace
drumming its fists on the verandah roof
cool housed sense of being inside
watching the quivering air

latent rain imaginary downpour
impossible to reach to within me

a blocked curtain of water is shimmering
in a way it's always raining in this dark
while here (again I'm sleepless, frustrated with it)
October's inland arid country night
grazes over the dry, still, quiet land
and, in pain without you –
literally, breathing pain and absence –
I've woken up and go outside

to watch how the empty paddock slopes
stretch out
as if they're sleeping shadow-bodies
able to luxuriate, curled over, in their star-dotted cool
forgetful of yesterday's heat – the wall of it –
which was blistering down
on unsheltered clay, on the yellow-flowering
fireweed and the already dead blond grass

The Price of Wind

In the age of catastrophes –
its dry creeks the length of decades –
the price of wind was on everyone's lips.
We farmed it like we were angels.

A lost sale was unspent energy
buffeting down the neighbour's paddock,
and the way it mimicked all the phrases
which human breath can play with. –

This wind's word, its unplantable seeds,
grew from despair and blindness –
the earth's despair, the eye's narrowness.
Nothing hovered in its invisibility.

When you drove down to check the dam,
the future was like that brief, shiny water.
Dark, pale cirrus was streaked in it.
Snake-necked turtles were laying eggs in the last green.

Gayle Kennedy

Bringin the old ones home

Me, Antman and Fleabag was travellin though river country and decided to stop by and spend a coupla days with his cousin, Jake. Ant and Jake was real close, they grew up together and was more like brothers than cousins. It upset Jake a lot when Ant went to live in the city. He followed him for a while but couldn't settle. Said he couldn't feel his blackness in all that concrete. Couldn't see the stars, smell the earth or hear the whisper of the old fullas when it was quiet and dark.

Jake was real in touch with bein a blackfulla. He could read the earth and knew before any weatherman when it was gunna rain, when you was gunna have a drought, all that kind of thing. He knew when trouble and sad times was comin too, cos the willy wagtails told im.

Anyway, this time we pull up and there's no sign of Jake. The front door's open, but he always leaves it like that in case someone needs a feed or a bed and he aint home. So we walk outside and old Mrs McCormack calls out to us. We wander over. She'd know, if anyone would, what Jake was up ta.

She gives us a big kiss and picks up Fleabag for a cuddle and tells us that there's been some sorry business. Jake's been asked to take care of things. She doesn't want to go into anything cos she reckons it makes her feel funny inside, but says Jake'll tell us when we see im. 'He's down at the old water hole,' she says, 'with a whole heap of other fullas.'

She tells us she's just seen Gus Hill walk past on his way to the pub with Jake's order. She reckons if we hurry we'd catch him and could fetch Gus and the supplies back out to Jake. It'd help everyone out.

Gus Hill is Jake's dog. A pure white little fulla cept for a big tan heart on one side. He was wanderin past Jake's, lookin scrawny, tired, thirsty and hungry one day and Jake called im in. He give im a feed and a drink and told im he could hang around if he wanted to. Gus took im up on the offer. He had a tag round his neck with the name Gus Hill on it, but no one ever come lookin for im.

Anyway, Jake taught im how to do lots of things and Gus seemed happy to go along with it for his room and board. Cos Jake aint got a car or a phone, he puts messages in a little pouch round Gus's neck. He's taught him to go to the pub or store with his order and they bring Gus back with it later and collect the money. Sometimes if he's too pissed to walk, he'll send Gus round to relations or mates with messages if he needs to yarn with any of em.

Anyway, we decide to go and pick up Gus and go out and see Jake. We tell Mrs McCormack we'll catch up with her later and cruise off.

We git down the pub and there's Gus sittin inside with a bowl a water and a snack. He's real happy to see us and makes a bit of a fuss over his old mate, Fleabag. The publican, Curley, comes round from the counter to shake Ant's hand and give me a kiss. He shouts us a beer and we tell im we'll fetch Jake's order out for im. We git out to the waterin hole and there's the biggest mob of fullas out there. Lots of kids and dogs, and lots of elders. Flea sees Jake and jumps outta the window and goes barrellin over to im. He looks real surprised to see him and grabs im and starts cuddlin im. We open the door and let Gus out and go over ta Jake. He starts cryin and grabs Ant and holds him real hard. Then he gits me in a bear hug.

'Whut the fuck you fullas doin ere?' he yells.

We tell im we was passin and thought we'd call by for a coupla days.

Ant asks im whut the sorry business was all about.

He tells us ta have a beer then we'd go for a walk.

Bout half an hour later we walk over to this mound and we sit on a log and he tells us the story.

'Some fulla out on one of the properties found a big heap of old bones lyin all together. He reported it to the police and they found out it was the bones of blackfullas who'd been shot round a hundred years ago. Anyway, the fulla felt real bad cos it woulda been his people whut done it. He went down to the Land Council and asked how he could set things right and they tell him he could have the bones reburied in the proper blackfulla way and if the old fullas whut died was happy, their spirits would come home to rest.

'So they come and asked me.

'I was real happy to do it. Those poor old ones' spirits would be out there floatin on the wind cos they died so violently. They must be buggered and need to rest in their own place by now.

'So I got together the mob and we collected the bones, and cleansed them in a smokin ceremony and wrapped them proper and reburied em and we had another smokin ceremony. Now we just waitin ta see if the old fullas are happy and comin home.'

Jake tells us to hang round if we want. We was real honoured to be asked and Jake took us to the burial place and we knelt beside the big mound and held hands while Jake sang a song in the lingo real quiet and soft. Gus Hill and Fleabag started to howl real soft too. It was scary and lovely at the same time.

That night we sat up eatin emu and johnny cakes and singin and yarnin. When ya went off into the scrub to go to the toilet you could hear the soft voices floatin on the wind. Later we all sat quiet. The whole place felt real peaceful. We could hear the river flow and the soft rustlin of the leaves on the big old trees. Jake reckoned the old ones would've sat under the same trees all those years ago. Then Jake told us all to not make a sound, so we went silent and suddenly we could hear the old fullas whisperin in the night. Jake reckoned they was happy and was on their way home.

Funny thing is, next morning we all woke up at the same time. We looked over and saw Flea, Gus and the rest of the dogs all lined up and lookin up into the sky. Their ears wuz all pricked. Next thing, we hear the biggest noise and look up and this big flock a cockatoos comes roarin over our heads and disappears into the sky.

Jake and everyone starts huggin one another and jumpin round. Jake comes over and grabs us both.

'They're home. The old fullas ave come home.'

We sure did celebrate that night. We invited the old farmer and his family along. Jake reckoned they really needed to know they done the right thing.

Sarah Day

Sky Writing

Things fall apart. Across a summer sky
the emblematic Coca Cola script
above the uproar, miles long, a mile high

dissolves like cirrus before the squinting eye,
until all that's left's a vaporous postscript.
Things fall apart. Across a summer sky,

once, subtler heavenly signs might testify
foreshadowing the end of Rome or Egypt
above the uproar, miles long, a mile high.

That titanium on blue could edify…
there's a lofty riddle to decrypt.
Things fall apart. Across a summer sky

now wind-drift pulls the letters all awry
the pilot banks, the plane signs off, wings tipped
above the uproar, miles long, a mile high.

See how the characters emulsify
into the blue, now vacuous, nondescript.
Things fall apart. Across a summer sky
above the uproar, miles long, a mile high.

Biology Class

Ms plumps a dead weight in a plastic bag
on each desk. She tells us we are about
to dissect the pluck of a sheep. The pluck
she says, consists of the windpipe lungs and heart;
she asks us to feel the trachea cartilage –
we are wearing surgical gloves; its ridges are like the rings
on a vacuum cleaner hose and to feel with our fingers
how far it branches and to notice how
when deflated the lungs appear to be dense
but when we cut off a chunk it floats in the glass beaker.
This shows what, says Ms, that it is full of air we chant.
Later we will hold the heart in our hands and see how
the right ventricle is larger than the left; we will insert
an index finger in the aorta – Laura Jones says guess what
this reminds her of – to see what volume of blood
gave life to the animal. Ms says to notice the strength
of the valves and the fine mesh of heartstrings
which are reinforcements holding together this dark red organ.
I run my finger tip along one sinew, it is like a violin string,
and think of that expression *tugging on the heart strings*
and think of loving hearts and broken hearts
and wonder if a sheep feels pain and sorrow and delight.
Now Ms is giving out lengths of clear tubing
to push into the windpipes; she instructs one girl in each group
to grasp firmly while another blows to inflate
the lungs. The group by the window – Laura's cacking herself,
has a pluck with its voice box intact. It bleats
like a lamb in a paddock. I keep hearing that maa
like a drawn out sigh and wonder
would its mother recognise this call?

Apples

These apples have weathered
the rise and fall of civilisations,

have travelled the Silk Route
from Khazakstan to ancient Persia,

have witnessed from bough and basket,
the matrimony of gods and the evolution

of the wheel. These sweet, rolling
pleasure-fruit, eschewing affectation,

consort of pie crust and dumpling,
ally of clove and nutmeg, still hold their own

on the twentieth century grocer's shelf.
Aristocrats, Democrats, Beggars and Kings

on a par in this assembly
where Early Joe will jostle in a bob

with Lord Derby or Prince Alfred
or Bedfordshire Foundling; while Beauty of Bath,

Maiden's Blush and Geeveston Fanny
are lines illustrious as any dynasty.

These russet, golden, red apples
of autumn, allies in sickness and in health,

with which we have kept company
since the Stone Age, toted from East to West

on sailing ships across the southern oceans;
these same apples which Eve's teeth

cleaved defiantly to sepaled eye
and scattering of seeds;

chaste reminders in sepia still-life,
alongside lolling hare and game bird,

of beauty and of vanity; whose volume
and space inclined the Cubist eye

and from whose plumb-line tumble
a new physics was conceived;

a wonder, that these half-dozen apples
on a plate are with us still, smelling of loamy cider

like uncollected windfalls. Think apple,
think of the rattle of loose seeds in a Cox's Orange,

or glossy green helices, and tart cookers
foaming in a pot, or the acid crack

of beeswax bloom and fragrant new-season flesh.
These half dozen apples on a plate –

currency of Everyman's pleasure.

Pat Hutchings

Protecting the Great Barrier Reef

Coral reefs are among the most diverse ecosystems known to man. They occur within warm tropical waters between the Tropic of Cancer and the Tropic of Capricorn, extending to depths of about 30 m. Below this there is insufficient light for the reef-building corals to flourish. Live corals are actually just a veneer of living tissue covering the reef framework, which has been built up over centuries. This reefal framework is a three-dimensional honeycomb structure, which has been created by animals and plants boring into the calcium carbonate substrate, and provides a home to a tremendous range of marine life. While considerable attention has been given to the corals and fish which initially attract the eye when you first swim over the reef, far less has been given to the animals and plants which live deep within the reef framework. This is where my research has been concentrated over the past three decades.

Most of the animals which occur in the reefal framework spawn into the water column, where fertilisation occurs; pelagic larvae may spend anything from a few hours to weeks in the water column, as plankton. This larva must then recruit onto a suitable coral substrate surface and bore down or find an existing burrow. If a larva happens to settle onto a living coral, it is likely to be eaten by the coral polyps. It is only when the coral dies, or when part of the colony is damaged, that larvae can settle. So my initial studies were to describe the fauna living in dead coral substrate. It was apparent that, over time measured since the coral died, a distinct succession of animals had occurred. Initially the dead coral surface is colonised by algae both on the surface and below. This conditions the substrate and makes it attractive to the larvae of a wide range of animals. Small worms, which can have short life cycles and rapidly build up large populations, are followed by bivalve molluscs and, later on, by sponges. Similar boring assemblages can be recognised in fossil coral reefs. The presence of the algae, both on the surface and within the first few millimetres of the substrate, makes it attractive to herbivorous fish, such as parrot fish, which take large bites of dead coral using their beak-like jaws and grind it up in their specialised stomachs, obtaining nutrients from the algae and excreting the calcium carbonate into the water column as a fine powder which then settles on the reef. Other grazers include sea urchins which, while relatively uncommon on the Great Barrier Reef, are abundant in parts of French Polynesia. They also use their teeth to scrape off the algae, taking with it some coral substrate. The term 'bioerosion' is used to describe the loss of calcium carbonate by both grazers and borers, a process which often makes the substrate more susceptible to physical erosion during storm events and may lead to large heads of dead coral being broken off and rolling down the reef slope, acting like bulldozers, and removing everything in their wake.

Once the substrate is extensively bored, it also provides home to a wide variety of animals – so-called opportunistic species. They cannot themselves bore, but they utilise the burrows created by the borers, which become vacant when they die.

In order to measure the rates of loss of calcium carbonate both by borers and grazers, I set up a series of experiments along a transect from the North Queensland coast, across the lagoon of the Great Barrier Reef and out into the Coral Sea. Along this transect, the amount of suspended sediment in the water column declines from the coast out into the clear waters of the Coral Sea, far away from any source of terrestrially derived sediment. The two sites closest to the coast were at Snapper Reef, located just at the mouth of the Daintree River, and Low Isles, which lies just to the south and within the flood plume of the river during the wet season. The catchment of the Daintree River is a fairly pristine catchment with only limited clearing upstream for cattle, but even so, after heavy rains during the wet season, plumes of terrestrially derived sediments are washed down the river out into the Great Barrier Reef lagoon, and cover the reefs of Snapper and Low Isles.

Regular-sized blocks of unbored coral were attached to the reef at six sites along the transect and sampled at intervals over five years. The study clearly showed the effects of sediment on the amount of substrate lost by either grazing or boring. Inshore sites, where the coral blocks were covered by a thick layer of sediment from the river plumes within weeks, reduced the amount of algae colonising the blocks, and therefore less grazing occurred. In contrast, at sites in the Coral Sea, where water visibility was often more than 40 m, rates of grazing were much higher; the clear water allowed the algae to grow rapidly. Conversely, rates of boring were higher at inshore sites than at offshore sites, although the type of animals boring varied between sites. The study clearly shows how this natural process varies between sites and the impact of increasing nutrients.

Working with my colleagues from Marseilles, we set up similar experiments in French Polynesia in the atolls of Tikihau and Takapoto, and on the high islands of Tahiti and Moorea. The site in Tahiti was close to the main town of Papeete and adjacent to the international airport. It is subjected to high levels of river-borne nutrients from domestic and industrial sewage. Extremely high levels of grazing were found, this time not from parrot fish, which have been almost completely fished out, but from plagues of sea urchins, which are removing amazing amounts of reefal framework. As almost no coral recruitment is occurring at this site, rates of loss of calcium carbonate far exceed gains from coral growth. Unless this situation changes, we are looking at complete loss of the reef framework and with it all the animals and plants associated with the reef. Loss of this protective fringing reef will mean that low-lying coastal areas will be far more vulnerable to storms. If this occurs on low-lying atolls, along with rising sea levels, it will make such atolls marginal places for human habitation. Loss of reefs also means that tourism and fishing will be severely affected and any source of income from these sources will be jeopardised. People do not want to dive on a dead reef dominated by algae and almost completely lacking colourful fish.

More recently my research has been focusing on the impacts of climate change and I recently co-ordinated a chapter for a Vulnerability Assessment of the Great Barrier Reef. This first regional assessment was a joint venture between the Great Barrier Reef Marine Park Authority and the Australian Greenhouse Office. We looked at increasing water temperatures, changes in alkalinity, rising sea levels, changing rainfall patterns, changing water currents and increased intensity of storms and the impacts of these factors on the invertebrates (excluding corals) living on or in the reef and in the soft sediments between the reefs i.e. in the lagoons.

While there is limited data for species occurring on the Great Barrier Reef, we examined examples from other areas and from the fossil record, in order to try and predict what might happen. The effects will vary between species groups and along the reef, with some species benefiting and others becoming losers. With increased frequency of bleaching of corals and resultant death of the corals in response to increasing water temperatures, we will see increased amounts of substrate available for bioerosion, leading to loss of reefal framework. Loss of live coral will certainly lead to losses of the fauna which live in between its branches and which cannot live anywhere else: an array of crabs and fish which are live-coral-dependent species which only feed on live coral polyps.

Some species will be able to move further south as the temperature increases, providing that there is suitable habitat for them. However, the southern tip of the Great Barrier Reef abuts onto deep water, so there is no suitable habitat for southern shallow-water species to move to. Oceanographers tell us that increases in temperature will not be uniform along the reef; rather it will vary, as will changes in rainfall patterns. Species already living at the limits of their temperature ranges will be most affected, while others may be able to adapt to rising seawater temperatures. It is also appears that while temperatures will rise, there will be times when water temperatures far exceed the average. These peaks have been responsible for the major bleaching events.

Increases are occurring at a rate which this fauna has never been subjected to, either in modern times or in the geological past. The fossil record reveals that entire coral reef communities have been subjected to temperature changes before. While some species have become extinct, others have survived to maintain coral reef communities over time. Skeptics use this as evidence that coral reefs will survive current global changes but my observations suggest that the rate of change is so fast that it is extremely unlikely any coral reefs will survive. In addition, coral reefs are being subjected to other anthropogenic inputs, such as increased terrestrial run-off, often contaminated with pollutants, such as fertilisers and heavy metals.

Rapid adjacent coastal development poses a significant threat to the reef. Mangroves and sea grass beds are being cleared for marina and residential development; upstream other sorts of riparian vegetation are being cleared. Mangroves and other types of freshwater riparian vegetation lining the banks of the major rivers which flow out into the Great Barrier Reef lagoon effectively act as kidneys straining the water as it flows down and trapping much of the sediment. Such loss of vegetation results in the river-flow not being cleaned, with dirty, contaminated water entering the Great Barrier Reef lagoon and changes to inshore reefs already apparent. Such communities, already under stress from poor water quality, are highly vulnerable to climate change.

Our review of the vulnerability of the benthic invertebrates (i.e. animals without backbones) stresses that climate change impacts will range from actual death of organisms to a variety of sub-lethal effects, such as the production of fewer gametes, reduced ability of molluscs to secrete shells, or crabs not being able to secrete new exoskeletons. This latter effect is as a result of changes in the alkalinity of the seawater. About 30 per cent of the anthropogenic CO_2 injected into the atmosphere since the Industrial Revolution has been absorbed by the oceans and this will continue until we substantially reduce greenhouse gas emissions.

Increased CO_2 in the oceans is changing them, making them more acidic, which leads to complex consequences for many biological processes that are influenced by ocean carbonate chemistry. These changes in ocean acidification will modify the rates at which corals and other calcium-secreting organisms can create new skeletons. This will mean that coral reef structures will be far less dense and presumably far more vulnerable to bioerosion. I am just about to start a project investigating this: we will be manipulating levels of CO_2 in small aquariums – mesocosms – and measuring rates and agents of bioerosion under varying levels of CO_2.

In the Vulnerability Assessment, we suggested that the more mobile species may just move further south or into deeper water, but attached species such as sponges, gorgonians, and sea squirts cannot move, and their survival relies on their larvae being moved into more favourable areas for settlement. It is still unclear how the regional currents will change, although certainly they will, so it is difficult to predict the long-term future for such species.

The ability of organisms to survive will depend upon other factors such as food supply predators. Many species spawn in response to changing water temperatures, but if they spawn earlier in the year and there is inadequate food in the water column, this will severely restrict larval survival.

It is obvious that the impact of climate change on the benthic invertebrates will vary according to the timing of events, such as when pools of hot water sit over the reef – if this coincides with a massive flood event, then it will be far more disastrous to those communities than a temporary increase in temperature, rapidly dissipated by water movement. Some of the migratory seabirds depend on these benthic invertebrates and we are already seeing declining levels of breeding success as the adult birds are failing to find enough food to feed the chicks, and are leaving them to starve on the nests on many of the islands of the Great Barrier Reef.

So what can be done to ensure the long-term viability of the Great Barrier Reef? Even if we stopped all greenhouse emissions tomorrow there would be a considerable lag time before levels begin to drop. Experts are saying ten to twenty years, during which time we *must* reduce our greenhouse gasses. At least Australia is now to sign the Kyoto Agreement – which is a start, but we need to act upon this.

In the meantime, the Great Barrier Reef Marine Park Authority has rezoned the entire Great Barrier Reef in order to ensure that all habitats are represented in 'no take zones', which currently protect about 30 per cent of the entire reef. I was one of the experts who formed a working group to identify the major habitats within this enormous park, which is over 2,300 km in length, and we identified seventy bioregions, thirty representing reefal areas and forty representing different habitats in the soft bottom, inter-reefal areas. These bioregions were then used as the basis for the zoning plan. For each bioregion where commercial and recreational fishing occurred, the boundaries of the 'no take' or 'green' zones, as they are also called, were chosen to minimise social and economic impact and a large number of commercial fishing licenses were bought out. This rezoning was approved by the Australian Government in December 2003, and came into force on 1st July 2004. While there was a lot of support within the community, there was also considerable dissent and much political lobbying was undertaken. As members of the Australian Coral Reef Society, we wrote to all politicians, both at State and Federal level; many of the seats along the Queensland coast were marginal, which always makes such lobbying interesting. We also went to Canberra to talk to Ministers, and finally, after months of fine-tuning of the boundaries, the Representative Areas Program (RAP) was taken to Cabinet. After they had agreed to support it as a complete package, it went to Parliament, where it was supported unanimously. The rezoning cannot be reconsidered by Parliament for seven years. No political party dared oppose the bill, as the Great Barrier Reef is a great Australian icon and people who have never even seen it want it conserved. Before the rezoning plan review, monitoring programs must be implemented to show that it is actually facilitating the management and conservation of the reef.

Surveillance of commercial and recreational fishers is being undertaken, the skippers of several boats have been brought before the courts on the grounds that they were fishing in protected zones. Commercial fishing boats must be fitted with Vessel Monitoring Devices, which allow the authorities to know exactly where the boats are and what they are doing. The courts have accepted these computer-generated data and several operators have received major fines. News of such events rapidly spread through the fishing communities along the reef and the number of incidences is declining.

Another thing which the Authority has done is to work with Queensland Government agencies to improve water quality and restore riparian vegetation along the river banks. This typically includes privately-owned land. The Government can try to convince such owners that retaining the riparian vegetation may enhance efficiency and develop ways in which land run-off can be reduced by better farming practices. This may result in fewer fertilisers being used, as less is washed off the land and out into the river and subsequently onto the reef. Such spikes of fertilisers in the water column are common offshore after heavy rains.

Hopefully, by improving water quality, reducing land run-off, reducing levels of fishing, and increasing protection the Great Barrier Reef will have the best chance to recover at least some sites affected by climate change. However, in the long term, unless drastic changes are made to greenhouse gas emissions, coral reefs as we know them are doomed, and with them a considerable chunk of marine biodiversity and one of the most productive ecosystems known to mankind. As a practising coral reef scientist, I and like-minded colleagues continue will continue to push the authorities to undertake the best possible practice in managing the reef for future generations.

Karen Knight

Inner Boxing

Our new neighbours know
the art of boxing.
After dinner, Dad sends his sons
to the double garage
to protect the family Holden.
He wants their bull terrier back,
the television set, Mum's leadlight
panel, stolen from the front door.
Dad wants his kids to feel safe
again, safe in the uppercut jab
of their sleep.
All night, the sound of technical
knockouts, pro-style gloves
against a freestanding heavy bag.
Our neighbours are going to punch
the Australian Dream into shape,
and put it back into their own backyard.

Gentle Annie Falls
Waterworks Reserve, Tasmania

The child was found with an open mouth
as if hungry for the picnic she had lost.
All those meat paste sandwiches,
the strawberries and Spanish cream.
With the blue groove of a gum leaf
she was playing boats beyond reach
when she fell with the waterfall.
Her velvet dress, splayed out
like a pinned, blue butterfly.
The local constable rocked the body,
felt the weight of a mother's grief.
For years he drank
from the gold-white water
until there was only rumour
lifting the whispers down
from the wild cherry trees.
A cautionary tale
for a century of picnics.

Big Blue Gum
Eucalyptus globulus

Lightning strike veteran
weakened by dry rot
the sky dropped its jaw
when your arms
full of birds
split apart
like a piñata.
As your giant trunk released
pre-flight parrots
arborists felt the vibrations
of a thousand songs.
Your glaucous green leaves
fell like feathers
branding the ground
with antiseptic scent.
Ring-tailed possums
thrown from their nesting cavities
wailed into ribbons of bark.
When the last of your living tissue
powdered the air
the aftertaste of your nectar
lingered.

Broken

How to play this drum
now the hide is torn
unpinned from the blackwood shell
the goat wounded again

now the hide is torn
it stumbles and can't get up
the goat, wounded again,
bleating for mulga country

it stumbles and can't get up
parchment-thin and limp
bleating for mulga country
this flat sound of sorrow

parchment-thin and limp
unpinned from the blackwood shell
this flat sound of sorrow
how to play this drum

Taking Stock of the Land
Photographs by John Kirk

Fleece Toss

Farmer and Sheep

Stockman, Queensland

86

Above: Homestead. Left: Shearing

Billy

Kim Scott

An Island Home

Last weekend a friend cooked me some abalone we'd plucked from the waters of one of the many bays along the south coast of Western Australia; one of those bays where you see the sun as it rises over the sea, or sometimes – depending on the time of year and where you sit – it rises over a strip of land beside that sea. It's the sort of place migrating whales sometimes strand themselves in, and in that way at least it's similar to the home of my indigenous ancestors a little further around the coast. So you'd think I'd know everything about its natural foods – its bush tucker. I don't. I was a bit embarrassed being shown how to prepare and cook that abalone.

You slash the strong, fleshy foot from the shell with a knife; next, scrub the sand and grit away, wrap a piece of cloth around the disc of sea-meat and bash it once or thrice with a hammer.

I'd stepped from the stale air of my motor car clutching eggs, a loaf of bread and some wine. I was looking forward to opening one of those bottles, but my friend insisted on me shivering in cold saltwater, bumping against slippery rocks, breathing through a gurgling pipe. I felt a bit like one of those stranded whales.

It seemed a very long time before we got to the wine.

I sipped further comfort from some research I'd been doing:

indigenous people – that means Noongars here – never ate oysters, despite their abundance in many sheltered coves. Ships' crews pausing to resupply couldn't believe their good fortune and, writing about it in their logbooks, created such imaginative placenames as… Oyster Harbour.

They taste very different to abalone, oysters. I don't rate either of them, really. Edible enough, and certainly healthy: but so is all bush tucker.

We were camping on my friend's bush block. It's sea-change and tree-change country all at once: a granite headland, freshwater springs and clumps of trees towering in the granite's shelter from the prevailing cold, southerly winds. Dense bush spills down the steep slope to a crescent of sand. A couple of small islands sit a short swim from shore, and there's deep water between.

It's a refuge folded into granite rock not far from where the southernmost part of mainland Western Australia dives into the sea. A boat was built here in the early days of colonial Western Australia, and one time it was a shore-based whalers' camp. Cosy Corner, they call it, this grove of peppermints beside the Southern Ocean.

To most readers, it must seem a very long way from anywhere; we'd driven several hours from Perth, a city regularly joined to the phrase 'the most isolated in the world'. The bland placenames might even sound familiar: Perth, Cosy Corner… then there's Torbay Hill, Port Harding, Perkins Beach… You could be almost anywhere in the English-speaking world, surely. And those two islands so close to shore? Richards Island and Migo Island.

I recognised the name of the second island, or something very like it. In the nineteenth century Sir George Grey mentioned Miago, a Noongar man who had sailed with Sir Charles Darwin:

> The officers of the *Beagle* took away with them a native of the name of Miago, who remained absent with them for several months. I saw him on the North-west coast, on board the *Beagle*, apparently perfectly civilized; he waited at the gun-room mess, was temperate (never tasting spirits), attentive, cheerful and remarkably clean in his person. The next time I saw him was at Swan River, where he had been left on the return of the *Beagle*. He was then again a savage, almost naked, painted all over… Several persons here told me, – 'you see the taste for a savage life was strong in him, and he took to the bush again directly'.

Let us pause for a moment to consider.

Miago, when he was landed, had amongst the white people none who would be truly friends of his, – they would give him scraps from their table, but the very outcasts of the whites would not have treated him as an equal, – they had no sympathy with him, – he could not have married a white woman, – he had no certain means of subsistence open to him, – he could never have been either a husband or a father, if he had lived apart from his own people; – where, amongst the whites, was he to find one who would have filled for him the place of his black mother, whom he is much attached to? – what white man would have been his brother? – what white woman his sister? He had two courses left open to him, – he could either have renounced all natural ties, and have led a hopeless, joyless life among the whites, – ever a servant, – ever an inferior being; – or he could renounce civilization, and return to the friends of his childhood, and to the habits of his youth. He chose the latter course, and I think that I should have done the same.

Our retrospective view makes Grey's limitations obvious, but his honesty and high opinion of the Noongar man, Miago, is also obvious.

Miago would've been out of his territory this far south, but so often a 'guide', a 'native constable', or even an 'Assistant to the Government's Interpreter', he was accustomed to transgressing boundaries. Even so, I don't think he would've named an island after himself. That island may have been named in memory of him, but he didn't name it. The placenames he knew came from the language and stories of the first people to, in Jared Diamond's phrase, 'create a society in Australia'. Well, this part of it, anyway.

In Noongar – Cosy Corner's first language – the word for 'island' often translates as 'heart' or even, sometimes, 'knee'. Similarly, a hill is 'head'. This suggests that potential in this instance, expressed in roughly human form, is implicit in the landscape. It's a potentiality, awaiting a catalyst. And I reckon the catalyst is language.

What better way to appreciate the deeply human heritage of a place than by the language indigenous to it, the words and stories of its first society? Such words might even help a young, immigrant nation graft itself to the many older nations and older histories above which it shimmers.

Can that be done with justice?

We know that considerable damage has been done to our natural environment, and to indigenous languages. The map of 'Cosy Corner' shows very few placenames in Noongar language, other than an island that carries what may be the name of a Noongar man. The language is itself endangered; it has few fluent speakers, although at least there are more language teachers now than a few years ago.

Our shared history could be interpreted as designed to ensure that descendants of first societies don't know their ancestral languages, and don't know the placenames or stories they offer. In recent years I've tried to play a small part in reversing this. I like to call it 'language regeneration', but some prefer terms like 'resuscitation', 'reclamation', 'revitalisation'...

For me it means working with Elders to record and transcribe their language, and to identify its connection to the natural environment. It means going through archival language material with people who carry Noongar language. This is never an easy process: there are wildly variant spellings, there have been scribes with tin ears, there are words that contemporary Elders don't recognise. All of which can make the process unsettling, and even threatening. But it's also a joy to retrieve the voices of family you never heard speak, and to contemplate what they thought and felt and knew; to contemplate their world with them.

I'd like to say a little about a particular example of this. First, some background: eighty years ago an American linguist – Gerhardt Laves – visited one of the towns along our south coast and transcribed the stories of a number of Noongar men. When he went home, he took his paperwork – their stories – and began a completely different career path. After his death some notes were discovered in his attic and sent back to Australia sometime in the late twentieth century. A local university made his handwriting computer-friendly, and organised a community meeting to appoint a couple of representatives to help work out a 'protocol' for how to return the material to its community.

This was not as simple as it might appear. We tracked down descendants of the 'informants'. Sometimes this was very successful: we found a son and a daughter. They'd never really known their father; he'd died when they were very young and they were brought up in missions. One of them was an Elder in another part of the country. The surviving son of another informant, now in his eighties, was a well-respected Elder in our own region.

If there were no direct descendants, we found nephews and nieces. In some instances we could only locate grandchildren.

Eventually, we had a group of people who were descendants of Lave's informants, and also respected and well-grounded members of the Noongar community. We named them 'senior contact people' and they comprised a 'reference group' of about eighteen people, including a language teacher nominated by the majority of the group because of her skills and family connections. I use the phrase 'the majority of the group' because there were disagreements among us, particularly whenever we broached questions like:

- Who do the language and stories belong to?
- With whom should they be shared?
- What is the best way to do that?

The original 'informants' may well have been a single community, but there were jealousies and rivalries within our reference group, some with a long history, and we couldn't agree on every 'senior contact person'. Sometimes this was because, even if there was a genealogical connection, and even if an individual was recognised and accepted by the wider Noongar community and perceived by many as an Elder, it did not follow that they were regarded that way by our small community of descendants, the reference group. Sometimes they, or an earlier generation of their family, may have been isolated from Noongar community in their youth, or even (allegedly) denied their Aboriginality and thus perceived to have not yet adequately restored their connection to community. In another instance, a person initially nominated as a 'senior contact person' and thought to be a direct descendant of one of the informants, was challenged by others in the group, who cited welfare files showing that her mother had been fathered by a non-indigenous man, not the man who had claimed her as his child, and was directly descended from one of the linguist's informants. It was an argument, in many ways, about paper genealogies versus community acceptance and cultural knowledge.

Ironic: our arguments were conducted in English; and were a painful reminder of how oppressed communities turn on themselves.

Some of us in that group call ourselves 'social activists', and rally around slogans of social justice and the rights of indigenous peoples. In some ways our disagreements were more difficult to resolve than disagreements with the non-indigenous community, and at times I wondered if we'd become so accustomed to polemic struggle and conflict that we knew no other way of interacting with others.

Frankly, it's tiresome to recall our disagreements and their blustering intensity. Quite rightly, people wanted to know the stories and more of the language. Understandably, people saw status in being the gatekeeper of such material.

In the end, inevitably, the written protocol was a compromise agreed upon by a community of descendants. Upon its completion, a few people broke away, along with the documents they'd claimed, and those who remained were probably a stronger community because of it.

I make it sound very political; in truth, I hope such disagreements prove to be part of a longer process of community healing. Yes, there were raised voices and argument, and yes, there were tears. However, it wasn't only anger that caused those tears. Receiving the stories of your father, uncles, ancestors – even in a form you can't yet understand – can make you cry.

Just holding a bunch of papers and plastic can strengthen your sense of who you are, and of continuity.

But is clutching them enough? Questions remain: Who owns the words and stories? Aren't language and stories communal? How, with justice, can these words be shared?

To a writer, publication seems the obvious answer. However, that would make the stories accessible to everyone, especially wealthy book-buyers with good literacy skills, two categories which feature, largely for historical reasons, few Noongar people. Therefore, publication might mean that those old-times storytellers speak to their own descendants only after everyone else has heard their stories of the place in which they live. Consider the historical context: indigenous people being displaced from land, dispossessed and disempowered. You wouldn't want publication repeating anything like that.

Surely, justice requires words and stories be returned to, and consolidated in, a community of descendants, and shared from there.

Nevertheless, our group remained interested in publication because it would provoke interest – both within and outside our community – in our heritage and language, and give an opportunity to initiate further projects.

We planned to publish only a very few stories, inspired by archival stories. This would involve three workshops.

The first was intended to give 'senior contact people' and their invitees an overview of the material and to make them more familiar with at least some of it. Hopefully, their enthusiasm and support would create enough momentum for us to succeed.

The second workshop was designed to give individuals an understanding of the principles of story illustration, and a further opportunity to become familiar with the selected stories.

The third workshop was intended to celebrate the return and consolidation of language and stories. We'd inform people associated with our 'community of descendants' of the process we'd followed, exhibit the art created by the illustration workshop, read the stories aloud, and give selected individuals – particularly those involved in formal or community-based education – photocopies of the texts and CDs of them being read. We hope this contributes to the 'return and consolidation' of the stories, encourages language regeneration, and improves career and/or employment prospects for at least some of our people by making them 'experts' on the stories before they're published.

The workshops would be part of the process of publication. Participants would gain a sense of 'ownership' of the stories, and we would gain some experience on how to conduct similar future projects.

The first workshop began with 'senior contact people' being presented with 'their' stories in booklet and computer-disk form. It was very emotional; recipients and many in the audience cried because of this tangible return of stories and language. It occurred to some people there that it was unusual for so many of us to come together, other than for the too-frequent funerals.

We'd gathered at a camp in the bush beside a river not far from the town where the linguist had collected the stories. At most there would have been about fifty people present at any one time over the course of the weekend. People came and went; cars left and returned with a different set of passengers.

Across the floor we'd spread large sheets of paper on which, using the linguist's alphabet, I had written some of the stories chosen by the relevant 'senior contact person' and myself. Beneath each word I had also written its approximation in contemporary Noongar orthography and an approximate English translation. One page at a time, I attempted to read them aloud to a small circle of Elders on chairs around me as others beyond that circle observed, wandered away, moved in closer. People gathered in small groups outside the room, talking about what was happening, speaking Noongar language where they could. Then they'd come back inside to observe a little more.

It was intense in that circle, working out those stories. We recorded the Elders correcting my mispronunciations, and also their elaborations and digressions. Sometimes there were words or instances of language with which the Elders were not familiar. Not that they always agreed among themselves. Some of my generation, moving outside the circle of Elders and into my vision, signalled a break using the basketball 'time-out' signal.

In 'time-out' they emphasised what I was only half-aware of: the circle of elderly people was being dominated by those few with good hearing and able to read the strange alphabet; some were competitive enough to confront their peers (let alone the deceased linguist and upstart workshop facilitator); others of a more gentle temperament looked like they were getting ready to slip away.

We started again a little later, and over the weekend the membership of the groups changed slightly from one session to the next. And so the weekend proceeded: elaborating from scrappy documents, recovering the sounds of an ailing language, imagining and realising the stories. Lines on paper faded; stories grew. We felt encouraged to continue with our plan, although one 'senior contact person' became upset going through her father's story, and so we withdrew it from the workshop process. It was just too much for her, she said, to be hearing her father's words.

For the second workshop we employed an established book-illustrator, Frane Lessac. We wanted another story-sharing opportunity, and a chance for people to get involved and try their hand at illustration. With luck we could identify illustrators for publication from among our own community.

At the third workshop... Well, as I write, the third workshop hasn't happened yet. Are we running out of energy? True, one of our core people is recovering from a kidney transplant, and others have taken on the care of even more family members. It's also true that we're doing this independent of institutional support and with limited funding.

We intend the third workshop to be a celebration of the stories and our process. We'll exhibit the artwork and read the stories aloud. We'll hand out paper copies and audio-recordings of the stories, and reiterate our process. We want our people to know the stories before they're ever published, to feel involved and complicit, and interested in participating in any similar, future process that leads to genuinely sharing our heritage with an increasingly wider audience.

A very significant part of that heritage, Noongar language offers a profound relationship with our natural environment and human history, and insights into another way of being. There's justice in hearing it from the descendants of the people who first created human society here, and in helping those voices be heard. Language must be shared to be alive, and speaking-and-listening is no crude giving-and-taking. It's more mutual: an investment in ourselves.

'Island Home' was first published in *Just Words? Australian Authors Writing For Justice* edited by Bernadette Brennan.

Tara June Winch

Extract from *Swallow the Air*

I remember the day I found out my mother was head sick. She wore worry on her wrists as she tied the remaining piece of elastic to the base of the old ice-cream container. Placing her soft hands under my jaw so as to get a better look at me, Mum's sad emerald eyes bled through her black canvas and tortured willow hair. She had a face that only smiled in photographs. She finished fixing my brother, Billy, also in an ice-cream tub helmet and sent us fishing. Puncturing the fear that magpies would swoop down and peck out the tops of our heads.

She shuffled us out like two jokers in her cards, reminding us to go to Aunty's house before dark, and telling us again that she loved us. The screen door swung back on its rusted, coastal hinges and slammed under the tension. When I looked back down the driveway she was gone.

Billy rode fast, his rod suspended in the distance like a radio antenna. My reel thread over my handlebars – attached with a small bag of bread mix, a flip knife and some extra hooks and sinkers that I'd got from school as a trade for Monopoly money. All was swaying with my slackened momentum.

The sand was stewing. I threw my bike with Billy's below the dunes of spinifex and headed for the point. From there I knew that I'd have the best view of the beach, deep into the surging breakers and practically standing on the locals' surfboards. Last summer I'd seen a turtle from the same spot; he immersed half his body – just to spit. Only a few moments he'd stayed, but it was long enough to remember his beauty.

Mungi was his name, the first turtle ever. They said he was a tribesman who was speared in the neck while protecting himself under a hollowed out tree. But the ancestor spirit was watching and decided to let him live by reincarnation or something. 'Anyway, using the empty tree trunk as his shell, he was allowed to live peacefully forever as a turtle.' Or so Mum would say. She had some pretty crazy ideas and some pretty strange stories about other worlds and the government and the 'conspiracies'. But the story about Mungi was my favourite. It was what she'd really wanted to say, she wasn't paranoid about a turtle.

I crept over the rock pools; the edges were sharp so you had to walk softly. Gazing down at every shale shape, contorting each footstep onto its smoothness. At the furthest rock pool, searching the ledge for my usual spot, I saw something strange. Draped over the verge was a silvery mould, like a plastic raincoat sleeping on the stone.

Sheltering over the eagled remains, I inhaled its salty flesh burning under the afternoon sky. The stingray's overturned body looked more like a caricature of a ghost than a sleeping raincoat. I stepped back, imagining its tiny frowning mouth screaming in pain. It'd not long been dead and I wondered if it had suffocated in the air or if this was only its mortuary. Either way it had swallowed its struggle.

I pulled it onto the rock ledge by its wing; the leathery shields made a slapping sound at my feet. I wanted someone to see my prize but Billy was way back on the shoreline, too far to hear a girlish call. There were three short cuts on either side of its body – where a rib cage would be. They were like fish gills, I guessed, for special breathing underwater. My forefinger slid down its stomach and stinging tail to the tip, tracing around the two thorns that stuck out at the end. In my mind I saw the tail whip across like a garden hose and poison me with a quick and fatal sweep. I sat further away, just to be safe, and thought for a long time about throwing it back in, though I decided it was best kept away from the living, best kept up here in the air.

Pain had boiled up under its swollen body; I could feel the stingray's fight in its last moments of life. It looked exhausted, like a fat man in a tight suit after a greedy meal. But I had pity for the ray; I saw only the release of the dead inside. Stabbing my flip blade through its thick skin, I drew a long gape down the underbelly. An orange sack split open, pierced in the cutting. Oozing paint like liquid, the colour of temple chimes, over its pale torso.

An angel fallen, lying on its back, was now opened to the sky. I was no longer intrigued by cause of death, loss of life. It had died long before I had cut it open, but only blood made dying real. No longer whole and helpless, the stingray was spilling at the sides – it was free.

I took up my bag, blew a loving kiss to what remained and returned to my brother, taking care not to step on the sharp-edged stones.

I remember the beach that day, still scattered with people; the sand had cooled with the falling sun. Blankets with babies and families in those half-domed, tent things. It was that time of the afternoon where mums and dads were getting tired and bodies could get no more bronzed. The entire beach would be packed up in minutes. Billy hadn't caught anything; just a handful of pipis lay in his hat.

'How'd you go, sis?'

I showed him my empty palms. 'You?'

'Just the pipis, maybe we could get Aunty to fry em up, ask her if she got any fish fingers too! Jeez I'm starvin.'

We carried our bikes to the taps and washed our feet. Billy's feet were so much darker than mine; he'd sometimes tease me and call me a 'halfie' and 'coconut'. We'd be laughing and chasing each other around the yard being racist and not even knowing it. I peered out past the bitou bush toward the point, following the pairs of surfers' legs disappearing over each wave. The sea was again a moving silver gull, mirroring sunset's embedded lilac. And I was again a child.

When we arrived at Aunty's house there was a police car parked out front, its wheels scraping against the gutter. There were no flashing lights, no siren. We tossed our bikes into the yard and Aunty leapt off the porch and shuffled us inside, just as Mum had earlier shuffled us out.

Her arms were sticky against my shoulders; she was shaking and sighing like sleeping through a bad dream. She sat us down at the kitchen table and opened the top cupboards, the ones with the barley sugar in them. Though she looked inside at the back walls only to gather her thoughts. She flung her head down, limp at the neck; still gripping the cupboard handles. Aunty cried a lot, it made Billy cry too. I thought she looked like Jesus, with her arms holding the rest of her up like that.

She sounded all broken up, like each word was important but foreign. 'Your mum – she gone. She gone away for a long time, kids. Me sista, she had to leave us.'

Aunty wasn't sure of the words. They'd never crossed her lips before, not when Mum went to the TAB, not when she went to Woolies either. I knew she was dead.

I took off the ice-cream tub still crowning my head, and stared into its emptiness. Mungi and the stingray floated around in my beating mind. I thought about Mum's pain being freed from her wrists, leaving her body, or what was left. Her soft hands overturned and exhausted. Tears fell into the ice-cream container, dripping off my eyelashes and sliding over my cheeks. Salt water smeared her handwriting of black marker – *remember*.

And I knew it was all right not to forget.

Mark O'Connor

The Ecology of Australia

There are few things more pleasing than the contemplation of order and useful arrangement arising gradually out of tumult and confusion; and perhaps this satisfaction cannot anywhere be more fully enjoyed than where settlement of civilised people is fixing itself upon a newly discovered or savage coast. The wild appearance of the land entirely untouched by cultivation, the close and perplexed growing of trees… are the first objects that present themselves… But by degrees large spaces are opened, plans are formed, lines marked, and a prospect at least of future regularity is clearly discerned.

(Captain Arthur Phillip, first Governor of New South Wales, describing the new colony, 1789)

When you, gentlemen, first got your estates, your ground was well furnished with beautiful shrubs. You ignorantly set the murderous hoe and grubbing axe to work to destroy them, and the ground that had been full of luxurious verdure was laid bare and desolate… No person of taste who has seen the rocks which border the shores of Port Jackson [Sydney Harbour], and the beautiful trees, flowering shrubs, rock lilies and other plants growing there indigenous in masses and groups, unequalled by the art of man, must but admire them. No rocky scene in England or Scotland can be compared with it.

(Thomas Shepherd, Australia's first professional gardener, 1830s)

Since 1788 the ecology of Australia's dry continent has been profoundly affected by the verbal filters through which Anglo-Celtic or English-speaking Australians perceive it.

Many of the terms they found for Australia's strangeness, like 'Down Under' and 'Topsy-turvy Land', were unhelpful, even silly. The best term was already in use for one of Britain's earlier conquests: 'the new world'. North America was the new world only in the sense that it was like the old world, being a sort of second Europe, with (thanks to a recent land-bridge across the Bering Straits) much the same trees and animals.

But Australia was genuinely new. It was hard for folk from the UK to understand its climates (forever precariously alternating between droughts and floods), its rivers that flowed inland and vanished, its eucalypt forests that seemed immemorial yet might burn to a cinder tomorrow, and its lack of topsoil (or of the rich glacial and volcanic sub-soils of other continents).

Above all, in its extraordinary biology, Australia seemed like a second and separate creation. Gone were the placental mammals of other continents (apart from a few rodents that had been rafted there, one of which was evolving into a sort of otter, plus of course the recently introduced dingo). In their place was a whole suite of marsupial grazers, predators, and arboreal animals. Plus platypus and echidna, two diverse survivors from an unknown era when mammals laid eggs. A symbol of Australia's otherness might be the bounding two-legged gait of the kangaroo, so different from that of European ungulates, yet clearly and robustly efficient.

Australia was, and still is, even though much trashed and abused, a treasure-house of biodiversity. Its biological regions vary from high mountain snowfields to tropical rainforests, and then to tropical, sub-tropical, and temperate deserts, sclerophyll forests, and grasslands. Indeed it was taken and settled by Great Britain partly for ecological or botanical reasons.

Sir Joseph Banks, a passionate botanist, paid £10,000 towards (and to be part of) Lieutenant James Cook's expedition that explored eastern Australia. It was Banks who some years later (in 1786) helped make sure that Britain's next colony would be in Australia, and at one of his two landing spots. He misinformed HMG that the climate of Botany Bay (Sydney region) was 'similar to that about Toulouse in the south of France'– though he knew that the real parallels in latitude were with North Africa. Intending colonists were fed a similar line. To this day Australia's first and most populous state is known as New South Wales (hereafter NSW) rather than, say, New Morocco or New North Africa.

The botanic riches of Australia probably lay behind Banks's recommendation. The lure of finding new species glittered like gold in people's imagination then – a point well made in David Attenborough's *Amazing Rare Things* exhibition, which was recently on show at the Queen's Gallery, Edinburgh. And Banks had a special interest in 'economic botany'. He understood, perhaps better than anyone else in Britain, how much the wealth and power (and the populations) of the empire depended on certain new plants that Columbus and others had found in the Americas. Beans, pumpkins, maize, pawpaw, potato, tomato, tobacco, peanuts, sweet potato, were already important; but Banks might have guessed the future rise of crops like capsicum, avocado, custard apple, passionfruit, rubber, blueberry, cranberry, asimina ('North American pawpaw'), tomatillo, pepino, cherimoya, quinoa, yacon, oca, pecan, naranjillo, hickory, casimiroa, feijoa, tamarillo, casana, cocona, and more. Once enough new-world crops had been added to the existing old-world range, there was a profitable crop for almost any region, from the acid peats of Ireland to the alkaline soils of coral atolls. The sweet potato, for instance, had led to the clearing and farming of much of upland Asia.

Union of these two crop-suites is still far from complete, even after 500 years. It was delayed by the old world's sluggishness in accepting new and often frost-tender crops. It became not an explosion but a sort of steady propulsion down the centuries behind humanity's rocketing growth. As the Australian National University geographer Michael Bourke points out, the modern world is still living off the dividends.

Banks might have been even more excited had he known the truth (which perhaps he glimpsed at Botany Bay). Australia is not, as the maps of his day suggested, a mere extension of SE Asia, but a drifting relict of Gondwanaland, and the world's most long-isolated habitable continent. Radically new crops and herds might come from such a place. Moreover, the separation between Australia and the much larger continent of Antarctica is quite recent. (One side of the Rift Valley produced is still visible in the spectacular cliffs of the Great Australian Bight.) If the innumerable lost species of Antarctica, which was not always polar, are to be found other than as fossils under Antarctic ice, it will be in Australia. What riches might Australia's vastness, once properly explored, bring Britain and the world?

The explorers did meet plenty of promising species. Australia had mound-building 'scrub-hens', which consort readily with domestic hens and lay excellent eggs a third their own body-weight. It had edible wombats and emus, almost begging to be domesticated—in vain. It had geese, ducks, and 'plains turkeys'. It had over a hundred edible fruits, including a collection of wild *citrus* and *rubus* as promising as any continent's. One of its so-called 'native grapes' *Tetrastigma nitens* was already comparable in size and flavor with the best domesticated grapes. It had delicious chestnut-sized bunya nuts, and heavy-bearing large-seeded acacias from whose seeds Aborigines made high-protein flour. It had wild grasses, unrelated to those of the fertile crescent, whose grains had long been a staple for desert Aborigines. Even its spectacular semi-edible 'kangaroo apple' *Solanum aviculare* was at least as promising a candidate for domestication as the original tomato, being productive, perennial and frost-hardy to boot.

The hungry settlers did eagerly sample 'native fruits', yet found most of them disappointing. In Asia monkeys and apes offer rapid dispersal for seeds, and trees respond by evolving large sweet fruits to tempt them. Most Australian trees relied on birds, and produced small acrid or sour fruits. Above all, the Aborigines who had occupied Australia for about 60,000 years (far longer than Europe has been habitable) seem not to have cultivated trees or developed varieties. It was as if the apple, instead of being steadily improved for millennia, had been left in the same semi-edible state as the rowan. By contrast in New Guinea, a part of the Australasian plate that became a separate island only about nine thousand years ago, agricultural societies did develop, and numerous crops were found. Sugarcane, taro, bananas and breadfruit may well have originated there.

Yet in every case the early settlers, faced with the problem of quickly establishing themselves in a harsh environment, preferred to use or adapt already familiar crops. They simply could not afford the many generations of selective breeding (even if they had fully understood the process) to turn wild plants and animals into reliable crops or flocks. The same globalisation that had brought the British to Australia was making it impossible for the world to adopt new crops, unless a wild fruit or grain was already comparable to what centuries or millennia of improvement had achieved with domestic species. (One need only consider the ongoing neglect of so many of the 'lost crops of the Incas', and of two of the world's finest fruits, cherimoya and feijoa.) Only one Australian species, the macadamia, a sub-tropical nut as good as domesticated hazels, proved immediately competitive.

Thus 'Botany Bay' became a receiver rather than a donor of new species. The settlers embarked on an orgy of often disastrous introductions: starlings, sparrows, mynahs, rabbits, foxes, trout, water buffalos, camels, prickly-pear cactus, and Scotch thistles (introduced by a sentimental Scot), and later two misconceived biological controls, gambusia fish, giant toads; plus the unintended stowaways: rats, mice, garden snails, and weeds galore… as well, of course, as more useful crops and herds. (One of the latest arrivals, courtesy of container shipping, has been the European wasp.) The settlers did adapt many of their new crops to Australian conditions. Famously, they replaced the UK's lanky wheats and stubby sheep with short drought-adapted wheats and long-legged merino sheep.

It was only in recent decades that CSIRO (Australia's premium scientific research body) set out to help some Australian species 'catch up'. They started with the desert quandong, a relative of sandalwood, that boasts an appealing cherry-sized fruit as well as an almond-sized edible nut. There were a series of steps: identifying economic potential, solving the problems of propagation by grafting or tissue culture, then having knowledgeable botanists collect cuttings or seed from promising trees across the species's wide range, and finally growing a large orchard of such trees from which one or more cultivars might be selected. The 'winning' specimen promptly became the world's most amputated tree, supplying twigs for hundreds of grafts. Quandong orchards are now in fashion, and many thousands of the new cultivar have been planted.

There have been similar successes since, most recently with the Australian desert lime *Citrus glauca*, both a good fruit and a promising rootstock for other citruses in dry or alkaline regions. There are many others – details can be found by googling 'bush food' – yet most of the new crops are as yet largely of 'boutique' or gourmet interest.

To return to the pioneers. Those who would soon call themselves the Australians found they now owned the partly unwanted and sometimes resented heritage of a stunning biological richness but one that was not much suited to feed or clothe humans.

Creating wealth and comfort involved introducing domestic animals, from honey bees (originally absent) to cattle, and destroying native ecologies. So began the age of introduced animals. Humans would in the long run prove the most damaging of these, with their endlessly expanding demands for consumer goods, food, and export earnings. Yet stunning damage was quickly done by three other early arrivals: fox, cat, and rabbit.

Early explorers reported dozens of small native marsupials, both herbivores and carnivores, that they saw every day: wallabies, bandicoots, potoroos, bilbies, quolls, numbats, 'hopping mice', etc. Within decades almost all had vanished – down the throats of introduced cats and foxes. (The selfishness of those who introduced foxes to mainland Australia, so that gentlemen could have a more familiar animal to hunt, has been surpassed only by that of those as yet unknown persons who recently introduced foxes to the island state of Tasmania – perhaps as a revenge on conservationists. It is also difficult to praise the Tasmanian politicians who did not then make fox eradication a priority.)

Yet predators, however efficient, need their prey animals, and can rarely wipe them out unless there is some other source of food. That source was the introduced rabbit, which bred unstoppably, having left behind its own diseases and parasites. The damage done by rabbit plagues is famous. What we may never know is how many plant species they wiped out as they ate the country bare. This went on till the 1950s when CSIRO introduced a lethal strain of myxomatosis, and then around 2000, as rabbits began to develop immunity to 'myxo', calicivirus. The rabbit plagues had a faint silver lining. Nobody starved in Australia during the Depression – though many got awfully tired of eating rabbit! CSIRO had another great success when it introduced the cactoblastis insect and saved much of Australia from vanishing under prickly-pear.

With fox and cat it seems it was the combination of *two* unfamiliar predators that drove most species to extinction. In Tasmania, in parts of the central deserts where foxes cannot find drinking water, and in parts of northern Australia that foxes seem to find too hot, many more small marsupial species survive. Elsewhere the small species vanished and were soon forgotten, but the big kangaroos that live in the open often proliferated as the land was cleared. Thousands of small dams, intended for cattle, allowed kangaroos to live permanently in the semi-arid regions, and exterminate many plants during the El Niño droughts. Kangaroo and emu became the iconic Australian animals, that hold up the Australian coat of arms. The 'real' mammal ecology of Australia had largely perished by 1900. Or perhaps it had vanished thousands of years earlier, when the diverse marsupial megafauna 'vanished' (as some prefer to say — though there is little doubt that in Australia, as on other continents, hunting by early humans was a major cause). The 'giant' kangaroos of today, a little under two metres tall, are really the babies of the kangaroo set.

The ecology European settlers encountered was already much modified, not just by the omnipresent Aboriginal hunters but by the fire regime they imposed. In Australia one should not ask 'Has this forest been burned?' but 'When was it last burned?' The dominant eucalypts ('gum trees') are what Californians have recently learned to call 'fire weeds'. Their inflammable oils create hot fires that destroy other species (and often themselves). Phoenixes of the tree world, their seeds usually germinate only after fire, and from their own ashes. The giant *Eucalyptus regnans*, the world's tallest flowering plants, reach sequoia-like heights in just 300 years. Yet they are dead of old age by around 400 years. 500 years without a major fire might see them extinct. But these are plants of semi-rainforests. For smaller eucalypts growing in drier areas, fire may be needed each hundred years, or fifty, or even ten!

The Aborigines obliged. In several regions they constantly set fire to the country as they travelled across it. They did this partly so they could always tell where the rest of a foraging band were, and partly to 'clean up the country' — to make it passable and to bring on green grass for the animals they hunted. (They also used fire as a hunting tool.) As a result, some researchers believe, dangerous large fires were rare, and the country was a varied mosaic of patches in different stages of recovery from relatively cool blazes. (The archaeologist Rhys Jones dubbed this 'firestick farming'.) Explorers often described the resulting effect as 'park-like', and imagined that it was natural. The numerous small marsupial species they found were the survivors that had adapted to these conditions.

Today those who seek to preserve Australia's forests indefinitely from logging and woodchipping are often accused of folly. 'If you don't harvest it, it will burn sooner or later, and the carbon will go into the atmosphere.' (Not that the loggers show much willingness to leave the 'old-growth' rainforests alone.) Fire-fighting techniques keep improving, but there is such a thing as 'fire weather', especially during Australia's El Niño years, when forest fires can be unstoppable.

I have taken a detour through 'economic botany' in part as preparation for a theme that runs through Australia's ecological history: the clash between the desire to protect biodiversity, versus the need of an ever-growing human population to make a quid from it. Australians are genuinely proud of their wildlife. They protect it, and allow only a handful of its species to be shot. (As a magistrate's son, I remember how often during the 1970s recent immigrants from Europe were up before the beak for assuming they could go out and shoot the birds 'for sport'.) Most graziers like having a few kangaroos on their property, and urban gardeners tolerate the nightly rampages and unwelcome prunings of the omnipresent brushtail possum — a protected animal. The extreme case of tolerance is found in tropical Australia where the once-endangered crocodile is now totally protected. As a result, its numbers have built up enormously, making it impossible for humans to swim in most inland or ocean waters — no small sacrifice to make in the hot tropics!

Another success story has been the 'high country' of the Australian Alps (aka Snowy Mountains) south of Sydney. This was treated as a communal stock reserve to which vast herds and flocks were driven in time of drought, with devastating results. The practice was stopped in NSW in the 1950s, but only much more slowly repressed on the southern side (in Victoria). Banjo Paterson's iconic poem 'The Man from Snowy River' (though it is not in fact set in the mountains) is regularly trotted out as proof that Australians will lose their heritage if the 'mountain cattlemen' are not allowed to graze the mountains.

Australia today has large national parks and is a world leader in managing them. *Protected Area Management* (Oxford University Press, 2001) by Worboys, Lockwood and De Lacy, an encyclopedia of the skills practiced by Australia's park rangers, proved so ground-breaking that in 2006 it was expanded and re-issued with the support of the IUCN as *Managing Protected Areas: a Global Guide*.

Yet habitats and species are vanishing. Bandicoots for instance. The mammal extinctions that occurred a hundred years ago in southern Australia are now, for reasons not entirely understood, but including no doubt the relentless spread of the imported toads, sweeping into the north. Tim Flannery has suggested that National Parks may no longer be the answer for conserving small mammals. Yet the vast effort by conservationists that has seen 10.7 per cent of Australia incorporated into a strategic network of protected areas will not be wasted. Under predicted climate-change some parks will become, at particular times, more important refugia than others for particular species, but all will be useful. The rangers have a fascinating project, called *Alps to Atherton*, to create linking corridors of natural vegetation, with the help of private landowners, between Australia's East-coast national parks, all the way from north to south, as a precaution against global warming.

Attitudes to Australia's biodiversity remain mixed. A group of giant kangaroos drifting across the landscape at speed, in a kind of effortless low-level pogo-ing flight, is an inspirational sight. But not if they are crushing, or eating, the crops by which you hope to make a living.

Many people in Australia assign a very high, almost religious value, to conserving 'nature'. Yet contrary views of the natural world as alien and threatening (for instance in the stories and news-dramas of children lost in the bush) are also widespread. So too is a developer's or industrialist's view of the natural world as a mere source of raw materials that is 'wasted' if not exploited. For instance the cosmologist Paul Davies has complained of Australia's Top End rivers 'going to waste' in that they are allowed to flow into the ocean, instead of being reticulated into a network of cities. (He forgot that the lucrative prawn-fishing industry would collapse if the wet-season floods no longer reached the sea.) A given individual may also hold different and incompatible attitudes on different occasions.

To describe the literary side of this story – the progression from authors like Henry Lawson who saw the landscape as monotonous 'bush' to those like Judith Wright who respected its complexity – would take another essay; but it is clear that a foreign tradition of appreciating landscape can be almost as lethal as none at all. Many who destroyed Australia's wonders were not immune to beauty, yet might have said like the poet Elizabeth Riddell 'But I was thinking of something English, out of a book'.

Can the fauna be made useful? Native-meat enthusiasts argue Australians should 'farm kangaroos' since they do far less damage per beast than hard-hooved cattle. But they also produce far less meat. 'Bush-tucker for a population of 21 million is nothing but a wet-dream (unfortunately), just like the delusion of continuous economic growth,' environmentalist Sheila Newman wrote recently. Kangaroo meat is lean, muscular and tasty, but often comes encumbered by Mylar-like bands of connective membrane called 'silvering' – very time-consuming to remove. Some people argue that farming the surviving kangaroo species would guarantee their survival by making them an economic asset. Others counter-argue that the population dynamics are too poorly understood. To commercialise kangaroos would leave their long-term survival at the mercy of those greedy for short-term jobs and profit.

Australia's beef, by the way, is mainly produced by grazing, rather than stall-fed on grain. In fact part of the case for vegetarianism is weaker in Australia than in the USA or UK, in that much of the grazing land is too marginal to have been used instead for crops.

Perhaps the most ingenious conservation initiative was that pioneered by John Walmsley, a maverick who kept foxes as pets to discover what kind of fencing could reliably keep them out. He stocked large cat-proof and fox-proof sanctuaries, like Warrawong in South Australia, with whatever rare and delicate small marsupial species could still be acquired from islands or zoos. It turns out that, thus protected, many of them breed like rabbits. There is talk of asking the Army to shoot out cats and foxes from certain peninsulas, which could then be fenced off, and thus gradually 'take Australia back from the fox' – as is already being done on the Peron Peninsula in Western Australia.

It might all have been far better if these predators had been kept out, and if, as Thomas Shepherd wished, wide borders of native plants had been left around each paddock, in a beautiful mosaic. But the first settlers, who were almost as many months from home-base as a settlement on Mars might be today, needed to grow food quickly or die. Decent old Arthur Phillip's duller eighteenth century belief in 'improving' the landscape prevailed. (Let us hope he enjoyed his retirement to Bath after he, as Les Murray puts it, 'recoiled into his century'!) Indeed land was often granted to settlers on condition they improved it, by destroying the native trees and vegetation.

This obsession with clearing the land may have reflected an unconscious need to eradicate traces of a prior Aboriginal ownership. Not that early settlers had the sort of bad conscience about having seized the communal lands of Aborigines that modern Australians have. The 'right' of a stronger country to seize a weaker one by *force majeure* was still widely accepted. The governors chose to believe the Aborigines did not own their tribal lands (which, in any case, delivered to European eyes little of value) because they moved across them like 'vagrants' rather than settling like European property-holders to cultivate and 'improve'.

Today we might prefer to praise the Aborigines' achievement in living sustainably with the land for millennia, and contrast it with the damage eight generations of European lifestyle has wrought. Yet in pre-1788 Australia you could not have found a horse, a wheel, a post office (or a literate person), an obstetrician… or bought an ice-cream, an apple, shoes, a piece of cloth, a pair of glasses, or a scone. The British were not wrong to think they were bringing a vastly smore complex material culture, or that the indigenes, even if they lost their communal lands, might still enjoy much improved material circumstances. (Even today, economists justify giving Russia's communal lands and assets to private entrepreneurs on grounds that these will then be more productively used, and that 'a rising tide lifts all boats'.) But the British fatally failed to understand the special cultural circumstances that might prevent a Stone-Age pre-capitalist society from embracing such opportunities. Or the drift of many Aboriginal groups, after losing their land, into the communal use of alcohol, a drug previously unknown in mainland Australia. (Alcohol, when a whole community adopts it, turns out to be not just a debilitating drug but a de-inhibitory one: it removes necessary constraints on anti-social impulses. The Australian media are currently convulsed with revelations about appalling levels of child sexual abuse in several Aboriginal communities.)

The British also made an ecological blunder, this time with creatures too small for them to see or even be fully aware of: human disease organisms. Should they have realized that, if they settled in Sydney, then measles, chickenpox, influenza etc would destroy Aboriginal societies and cultures? They had already seen epidemics follow ships' visits to Pacific islands. Yet Australia was not an island; and elsewhere in mainland Asia (and Africa) it was the Europeans rather than the 'natives' who died like flies upon first contact. The early governors did not know that Australia's thinly populated interior impeded the spread of epidemic diseases from Asia, and had left the southern Aboriginal populations with little more immunity than dwellers on remote islands. To their credit, they set up a quarantine station at North

Head near Sydney (its macabre history is now a tourist attraction) and largely succeeded in keeping the major epidemic diseases out of Australia. But minor diseases, not considered justification to prevent a ship landing, often proved just as deadly to the Aborigines.

It became widely assumed that Aborigines were 'a dying race' – a view that is sometimes dismissed today as 'wishful thinking' or prejudice, or as partly a cover for illegal killings. Perhaps it might also be described as ignorance of Darwinian selection. When three-quarters of a population dies within a few decades, largely it would seem of diseases for which no remedy was then known, one would naturally anticipate extinction. But the survivors may be those with more disease-resistant genes. In the south, a rapid intermixture of European genes probably speeded the process, and today Aborigines in the south (less often in northern Australia) often look racially more European or Asian than Aboriginal. It is now widely accepted that Aboriginality must often be defined in cultural-and-ancestral rather than narrowly racial terms.

Once the colony could feed itself fairly well, the next problem was to find an export to pay for its existence. In later days it was said that 'Australia rode on the sheep's back'; and indeed wool was an excellent non-perishable export, one that could be carried by slow unrefrigerated ships. It could also be produced from infertile land with a small labor force. But in the colony's first decades it was not the sheep's but the seal's back it rode upon. Skins stripped from the hapless Australian seals made excellent winter coats for folk back in the UK; and, then as now, most customers did not inquire into the ecological cost of a bargain. That industry was soon exhausted.

Then in the late nineteenth and early twentieth centuries there was the rise of wheat. Wheat itself had been grown in Australia since 1788, but it was labor-intensive, and phosphate-hungry. Yields tended to drop as soil fertility was exhausted. To counter this, much ingenuity was applied in creating better varieties for Australian conditions, and better crop rotations. Stump-jump plows and imported fertilisers helped. Then came the new fuel-driven machines. These made it possible to clear vast acreages, and then to mechanically sow and harvest them. Trains and steamships were now available to get wheat to markets around the world.

'Banjo Paterson' (1864–1941), author of Australia's unofficial national anthem *Waltzing Matilda,* hymned this re-born crop in his 'Song of the Wheat' (1914), ending:

> Princes and Potentates and Czars,
> They travel in regal state,
> But old King Wheat has a thousand cars
> For his trip to the water-gate;
> And his thousand steamships breast the tide
> And plough thro' the wind and sleet
> To the lands where the teeming millions bide
> That say: 'Thank God for Wheat!'

To this day, some councils and local progress associations give out illustrated books in which each line of Paterson's short poem takes up a page.

Imported 'superphosphate' improved Australia's infertile soils, but with time many soils have turned dangerously acidic. Wheat's fuel-bill includes nitrate fertilisers (made from fossil fuels), plus fuel for machines and remote-area transport. So far from being solar-powered, Australia's wheat industry works on a trade-off between the price of bulk wheat and the rising price of fossil fuels.

Today, despite its largish acreage and its specialisation in this crop, Australia produces only about 20 million tonnes a year, which is roughly 5 per cent of the world's wheat – though its willingness to export means Australia provides more like 20 per cent of a hungry world's wheat imports. Boomers who claim Australia could feed a far higher resident population forget the need to export most of the wheat to pay for fuel and fertiliser.

Australia's wheat farmers are skilled users of technology; and as yet yields are creeping upward, to over 2 tonnes per hectare in years with good rainfall. However many foresee future falls in yield, due to acidification, climate change, and soil loss. Every tonne of wheat is said to cost some tonnes of eroded soil. James McAuley wrote scathingly of how

> Flood fire and cyclone in successive motion
> Complete the work the pioneers began
> Of shifting all the soil into the ocean.

Even the patriotic poem known to all schoolchildren, Dorothea Mackellar's 'My Country' (1906):

I love a sunburnt country,
A land of sweeping plains,
Of ragged mountain ranges,
Of drought and flooding rains

could not turn a blind eye to

The stark white ring-barked forests,
All tragic to the moon

As well, much of Australia's farmland lies upon the bed of an ancient sea. Farming (and especially clearing) raises the water table and brings the salt to the surface. Paradoxically this dry continent suffers from rising salty water.

Two maps drawn by Chris Watson, a CSIRO soil scientist, reveal much about Australia's dependence on wheat. The first is a map of the areas of Australia that have good and poor soils for agriculture. As expected, only a few areas are classed as good. The second is a map of those regions with sufficient and reliable rainfall. Again, the good areas are relatively small. But what is really striking is the map produced by superimposing the two. Areas that have *both* deep fertile soils and reliable rainfall (like the area around Robertson in NSW where *Babe* was filmed) are not small, but tiny.

So how does Australia manage to feed its own 21 million humans, and export enough calories for about another 40 million? The answer, of course, is wheat. Not wheat grown on fertile soils with good rainfall, but drought-tolerant wheats grown as a winter-and-spring crop in areas where the soil is just middling, and the rainfall, during winter-spring, is usually enough – except in an El Niño year. And even so, the yields per hectare are lowish. Thanks to wheat (and refrigerated meat) Australia is a food-exporting country; yet in a good year it still grows less wheat than France – and in a bad year it sometimes grows less than Britain! A small return, perhaps, for so many square kilometres of fascinating bioregions cleared, and species locally eliminated or totally extinct. (In Australia as elsewhere, it is often semi-arid land, like the famous wildflower belt near Perth, that has the highest diversity of plant species. Nature, like humans, is at her most ingenious when stressed.)

Even more destructive than wheat, within Australia's relatively tiny rainforested regions (originally about 2 per cent of the land area), has been sugarcane – another economic success and ecological disaster. But for this profitable crop, most of Australia's lowland rainforest would still be standing. Instead only fragments survive. Fertiliser run-off from the canefields now threatens the Great Barrier Reef.

A certain distinction may be drawn between the north and the south of Australia. In the south swamps and wetlands were ruthlessly drained, and birds that might damage crops like brolgas (the famous giant dancing crane) and magpie geese were exterminated. The north was less suitable for agriculture, not so much because it had less water as because the water was concentrated in a few months. It is hard to farm flat land that is under water for three months of the year, and dry as a cracked scone for six.

Thus there emerged a sort of *de facto* agreement to leave the north more natural. Northern Australia's savannahs and seasonal wetlands are one of the globe's biological hot-spots. Some sacrifices have been made to keep them. For instance, the giant Ord River dam was intended to grow rice, but it soon became clear that this would mean exterminating most of the region's migratory flocks of magpie geese (a major tourist attraction). This had been done down south, but was considered politically unsafe, so less profitable crops were grown instead.

Yet even this agreement to spare the north is precarious. Climate change is expected to shift the rain to the north. Already the conservative senator Bill Heffernan has begun agitating for Australian farmers to re-pioneer the north. Predictably, some see him as a man of vision! However, the uneven spread of rain through the year may defeat his faith in the wet north.

Australia was a convict colony, not a utopian settlement. Governor Bligh (of *Bounty* fame) who suffered the 'Rum Rebellion' in Sydney, was the first of many to discover the near-impossibility of upholding long-term policies against the short-term interests of an emerging plutocracy.

By the mid-nineteenth century, Australia's press and much of its public life was dominated by the 'boomers', economic progressives who believed

Australia must and would rapidly acquire a population (and hence a status) comparable to that of the USA, or Europe. As late as 1978 I can remember seeing a large poster outside an Australian Embassy in which the outline of Australia was superimposed upon most of Europe, with the relative populations written beneath. The dry salt lakes of Australia's desert centre had been painted a vibrant blue, and the ephemeral inland rivers were thickly depicted.

The message was clear: *Come to Empty Australia.*

The great geographer Griffith Taylor, when professor at Sydney University, had a blunt answer for such nonsense. He produced maps with Australia turned upside down and superimposed on Saharan and sub-Saharan Africa – a better fit in area, and in rainfall and soil-fertility. He also told the boomers, correctly, that Australia's population at the end of the twentieth century would be not 100 million, as they predicted, but around 20 million; and that the 'boundaries of settlement' would not change much. Indeed, if anything, farms are retreating.

But the debate on Australia's population-carrying capacity is far older. Captain Cook, not normally a careless observer, remarked that on the coastal plain between Botany Bay (Sydney) and the then-impassable barrier of the Blue Mountains there was pasture for more sheep and cattle than could ever be brought there. Yet 20 years after settlement the herds were almost starving, and the authorities were desperately seeking a path through the Blue Mountains. Once the settlers broke through into the interior, the old pattern of complacency, followed by disappointment and ecological collapse was to be played out again, region by region. Exaggerated estimates of carrying capacity were always the first step.

Fire followed by rain can produce a flush of seeming fertility, but Australia's ancient stable continental plate lacks fertile volcanic soils – and mountains to bring down the rain. Its greatest river, the Murray, sometimes fails to reach the coast, and carries less water in a year than the Mississippi in a day.

'They call her a young country, but they lie,' wrote the poet A.D. Hope:

She is the last of lands, the emptiest,
A woman beyond her change of life, a breast
Still tender but within the womb is dry...
Her rivers of water drown among inland sands.

Only 6 per cent of the vast land mass has proved arable. Above all, Australia is intensely affected by El Niño years which bring savage droughts.

Thus Australia has played an odd role in the story of world population. Many a 'ten pound Pom' escaped from squalid conditions to a happier life in Australia, as did millions from the wrecked cities of post-WWII Europe, and more recently from Asia. Yet the total numbers that Australia could take in were globally insignificant. Worldwide, Australians probably did more harm than good by spreading the myth that the globe could not have a population problem, since there was still a huge 'empty continent' wanting more people. 'Land without people for people without land', as a Catholic bishops' conference fervently proclaimed. (In reality, Australia's agricultural frontiers had effectively closed by the time the colonies achieved federation and independence from Britain – simultaneously – in 1901.)

Australia has long been a talking-point in the debate between proponents of endless 'growth' and Malthusian 'limiters' – because it was one of the two new continents that Britain seized, thus invalidating or postponing Malthus's prediction that his motherland would soon run out of farmland for its expanding population.

Today the first group are typically economists who believe humanity can never run out of 'resources' because the 'market' will always find either cheaper means of supply or substitutes. Or else science will produce a breakthrough. (There is no faith in scientific miracles like a growth-economist's faith!) Their opponents are typically biological scientists who see limits to the numbers of humans – and the lifestyles – that a finite planet can sustain.

The well-planned South Australian colony saw a major battle between nineteenth century boomers and authorities. As the colony expanded into the increasingly arid lands north of Adelaide, its surveyor, George W. Goyder, drew careful maps of the rainfall and established a line (corresponding to 30 cm annual rainfall) beyond which land would not be offered for farming. The boomers were indignant at 'Goyder's Line'. How could Australia grow into a second USA if there was only room for a few hundred farmers in their state! Lines on the map were arbitrary, they thundered, and a barrier to human Industry. God would provide. Besides, it was a well known geographic fact that 'rain follows the plow'.

Following unusually wet seasons in the 1870s, settlers broke down the authorities' resistance and surged across Goyder's Line. A nobly-planned town, significantly named Farina, was constructed, as well as a railway line to carry off the anticipated huge harvests of grain – which never came. Today Farina is a sand-covered ruin.

But boomers never learn, especially when there are fortunes to be made on the mere expectation of growth. In the 1960s the giant state of Western Australia had a policy of clearing a million acres of 'scrub' a year. (In Queensland and NSW, even rainforest was called 'scrub'.) Advice that much of this land was species-rich yet marginal for agriculture and likely to be destroyed by salinity was ignored, with disastrous results.

The myth of the empty land was even written into the national anthem 'Advance Australia Fair' (adopted in the 1970s) which includes the words (against proudly swelling music), 'For those who've come across the seas:/ We've boundless plains to share' – a nice ideal, but a lie. Immigrants since the 1890s have not, in general, found farmland in Australia, and have paid through the nose even for housing land.

Till recently Australia's parliament has been one of the last preserves of the global warming skeptics and the 'nuclear will fix everything' illusionists. Local and even national newspapers run a depressing spiral of puff pieces about how we are desperately short of skilled and willing workers – alternating with pieces on how we are desperately short of major projects to provide employment. The intended solution is of course an endless cycle (or spiral) of increasing population and increasing construction. If only politicians could give Australia the construction industry its population needs, rather than the population its construction industry would like!

Yet the boomers did not have it all their own way in the twentieth century, as environmental awareness grew. In a single year, 1966, three environmental classics appeared: Jock Marshall's *The Great Extermination: A Guide to Anglo-Australian Cupidity, Wickedness and Waste*; Vincent Serventy's *A Continent in Danger*; and Alan Moorehead's *The Fatal Impact: The Invasion of the South Pacific 1767–1840*. Three years later the polymath farmer and environmental historian Eric Rolls produced *They All Ran Wild, The Story of Pests on the Land in Australia*. Another of his books, *A Million Wild Acres*, showed how complicated might be the series of ecological changes, even since 1788, that had created a particular terrain.

Three decades later the boomers came up against one of the few politicians brave enough to oppose them. Bob Carr was Premier of NSW from 1995 till he retired in 2005, the longest continuous term served by any NSW Premier. A brilliant and bookish man (he once stepped down for two weeks to attend Sydney Writers' Festival) he overcame the media's refusal to discuss the issue by himself writing and publishing full-page articles in the *Sydney Morning Herald*. In one he wrote:

> First, we need a democratic consensus on population. We mustn't fall for the line that more is better. A strong, proud and confident Australia doesn't mean a bigger Australia.

> Those who advocate an Australian population of fifty million aren't talking about the verdant stretches of cultivated land in the central tablelands or the western plains, let alone in the continental interior. They aren't talking about inland cities, conjured into being by benevolent developers and the Burley Griffins of our time. They are talking about the urbanisation of the eastern coast from north Queensland to Melbourne: ever more housing estates, more shopping malls and multiplexes, more freeways and petrol stations where now we have rivers and forests, unpolluted beaches and open country, and in a few areas (such as Daintree or Dadgee) coastal wilderness as old as the continent itself.

But Carr was one of a kind: a skilled politician, erudite, environmentally aware, and largely immune to the unsubtle tactics of the growth lobby, since he had no rivals inside or outside his party. The other state politicians have all caved in to the growth lobby, though some feebly protest. Former Olympic gold medal runner Ron Clarke, now the mayor of the Gold Coast (south of Brisbane) where rainforests turn into shopping malls overnight, has long been pro-development. Yet he recently mused in print:

> Where will the water come from for an extra 500,000 people on the [SE Queensland] Coast, and more than a million in the southeast?
> How about the roads, public transport, our open spaces, parks and gardens and our beaches – will they support a doubling of our population in such a relatively short time?

Not only farmers but politicians who ignore Australia's realities sometimes perish. The formidable conservative prime minister John Winston Howard, who ruled from 1996 to 2007, discounted talk of global warming, refused to sign the Kyoto agreement saying it would 'only destroy Australian jobs', encouraged uranium exports, talked of going nuclear, provided 'baby bonuses' and committed the Dry Continent to relentless population growth. It was his misfortune to fight the November 2007 election at the end of a disastrous drought, with cities running out of water, housing prices (fed by exceptional population growth) going through the roof, and with every week bringing fresh evidence that global warming is a reality. He boasted of a booming economy (based on his policy of selling off the continent's minerals and natural gas as fast as possible). No previous Prime Minister had ever lost an election in unambiguously buoyant economic times. Yet Howard was tossed out of office, even losing his own seat. The new Labor government of Kevin Rudd has had the good luck (like the Hawke Labor government in 1983) to come into office just as a crippling drought ended.

In the recent words of Ross Garnaut, Professor of Economics at the Australian National University, 'Australia is likely to be damaged more than any other developed country by climate change. Our climate is dry and highly variable already, and this will be exacerbated with climate change, with the effect on agriculture and water supplies being particularly pronounced.'

Australia's boomers remain unrepentant. Today they pay only lip-service to the myth of an empty continent awaiting farmers. They know the real money is to be made from the housing market, which is really the urban-land market.

It is a seeming paradox that such a huge country should have urban housing prices comparable to New York or London. Yet land area is irrelevant. Australians no longer found new cities; and granted the huge distances between major cities, the squeeze is on for inner urban land in Melbourne, Sydney, Brisbane, Perth, and Canberra. Throw in out-of-control population growth proceeding currently at 1.5 per cent a year (higher than Indonesia next door – or than many other third world countries) and the result is sky high land prices, which sometimes double in a decade.

These are always called 'housing prices' in the Australian media, but in fact construction costs are steadily falling. It is the price of land that is out of control. Each major influx of population kicks the housing market into another boom-cycle. Apart from moving any given greenhouse target further out of reach, the high cost of housing creates a huge invisible impost that swells the price of everything in Australia: goods, services, and labour. The huge unearned incomes to be made from real estate speculation in turn drive the population-growth lobby, in a python-like vicious circle that is the despair of environmentalists.

In the last days of 2006 the *Sydney Morning Herald* reported that Sydney's councils had been instructed to accommodate an extra 1.1 million people within 25 years. Each was given a quota:

> Densely populated Strathfield Municipal Council is expected to accommodate 9000 new dwellings – double what it considers possible … A spokesman for Bankstown Council said it had been set a total of 26,000 extra residences, which 'would have to be built entirely in place of existing homes.'

The task of maintaining any of Sydney's once-impressive environmental amenities against such pressures can well be imagined.

Rapid population growth has long been recognised as central, also, to Australia's ecological troubles. Those who resent suggestions that human beings can ever be a 'problem' sometimes claim that 'the real problem' is not human numbers but levels of consumption. But there is at present neither realistic likelihood nor intention of reducing per capita consumption. On the contrary, Labor and Conservative governments compete to assure the public that their economic skills will deliver ever higher affluence.

A November 2007 UN report classes Australians as even worse than Americans as greenhouse polluters, in fact the world's worst, producing about 26 tonnes of CO_2 per person per year.

Hence a series of Australia's official *State of the Environment* reports have insisted that it is essential also to curb population growth. Tim Flannery, who dealt with such issues in *The Future Eaters*, has speculated that Australia in the long term may be able to support only 5 to 12 million people – as against some 21 million now, and an expected 31 million as early as 2050. (The Australian Bureau of Agricultural Resource Economics agrees that production may fall steeply.)

Growth economists tend to pooh-pooh claims that Australia needs to feed its own people, and argue that 'The market will cope. You can always buy food.' They may be right. Australia's large area may not produce as much food as some believe, but it possesses mineral deposits (including natural gas) that took all earth's history to create but which it is current government policy to dig up and sell off rapidly. The resulting export earnings should allow Australia to import whatever food it needs – at least in the short term. Whether this is a good thing for the world is another matter.

The most recent book on Australia's ecology, *On Borrowed Time: Australia's Environmental Crisis and What We Must Do About It* (CSIRO/ Penguin, 2007, by David Lindenmayer, Professor of Ecology and Conservation Science at the Australian National University) makes some strong points. Like another professor of science, Ian Lowe, who heads the main conservation body, the Australian Conservation Foundation (ACF), Lindenmayer blames 'the three O's: overpopulation, overdevelopment, and overconsumption.' He is appalled by the recent decision to dam the Mary River in Queensland, home of the rare 'living fossil', the lungfish, so as to provide water for Queensland's ever-expanding human population. Australia, he says, 'leads the world in recent mammal extinctions… It is one of the most species-rich places on the planet. It also has one of the worst records of species loss and decline in the world. Almost no Australian resource-based industries can be considered to be ecologically sustainable.'

Yet he sees hope in paying farmers to reward them for 'better managing their properties for 'public good outcomes' such as revegetation, increased biodiversity conservation and improved water quality'. Indeed one major state, Victoria, over the last 15 years has turned its agriculture from greenhouse negative to greenhouse positive, largely through encouraging private owners to re-afforest their properties. In this, governments have been helped by better public attitudes (e.g. the 'Landcare' movement among farmers) and by long-overdue laws that restrict clearing of native vegetation.

No great attempt has yet been made to make immigrants – or the Australian-born – aware that residing in Australia is a privilege that should involve an obligation to conserve its unique species. The Howard government in 2007 introduced a citizenship test, similar to that in the USA, whereby applicants for Australian citizenship must demonstrate some basic knowledge of the country's traditions and political system. Donald Bradman is on the list of items they are meant to know; but inexcusably they are not required to know about the arid nature of the continent on whose fringes they are living.

Indeed many immigrants know only the well-watered coastal cities, and don't understand what the problem is about bringing in their mates. Some even believe such concern is just a cover for racism –in Australia as in the USA the word 'racism' is rarely used in its strict sense (referring to theories of genetic racial superiority) but has become a loose pejorative term for any kind of ethnic or national chauvinism that is disapproved. In this case it becomes, in practice, a way of crying wolf about a factitious issue while not attending to a real one.

Mind you, a tendency to cling to the coastal rim is equally visible among older Australians. James McAuley once described Australia as

> Bone-dry itself, with water all around.
> Yet as a wheel that's driven in the ruts,
> It has a wet rim where the people clot
> Like mud; and though they praise the inner spaces,
> When asked to go themselves, they'd rather not.
>
> James McAuley, 'The True Discovery of Australia'

The Whitlam Labor government of 1972–75 reacted to the first global Oil Shock by seeking to limit immigration and population growth and to borrow heavily to buy back Australia's energy resources for self-sufficiency. It was brought down by fierce criticism from business lobbies and media barons, and was the last Labor government to be critical of business or to think that ideals could matter more than economic growth. The incoming conservative government of Malcolm Fraser promoted indefinite growth, ignored energy constraints, and was made to seem prescient by the easing of the oil shortage.

All recent governments have favoured the flogging off (to China, Japan, the USA, etc) of Australia's (very limited) oil and gas fields as fast as they are discovered. This lets the current government boast of running a surplus, being 'sound economic managers', etc. Democratic leaders are ephemerids who know they are unlikely to be around in ten years time, unlike dictators who sometimes make better energy choices because they expect to be around for ever. Sadly, Australian experience shows that democracy is not good at preserving other species – they don't vote. It is also very bad at conserving resources.

The issue of population returned to haunt the Hawke–Keating Labor governments of 1983–1996. By now Australia was clearly a plutocratic democracy. The voters got their Hobson's choice every three years in free and fair elections between two major parties that jostled for the middle ground; but both parties competed for and depended upon 'electoral donations' from big money, and saw themselves increasingly as servants of the business-growth lobbies. The battle to ban media monopolies was effectively abandoned, with both parties selling out their own laws in hope of short-term political favours from media barons.

Hawke's dilemma was that Labor was using the conservation vote to cling to power, yet he dared not offend the growth lobby. The Australian Democrats Party, which often held the balance in the Senate, had a policy of zero net migration, and conservationists were demanding something similar from Labor. Instead Labor had pushed immigration ever higher, till only Canada had a comparable per capita immigration rate, and the polls showed the public was unhappy. In one poll in 1991, 73 per cent of voters said that the numbers coming in were 'too many' and, in 1996, 71 per cent were still of this opinion. Only 4 per cent thought immigration was too low. Clearly even Australia's large immigrant communities thought the point of sanity had been passed, though much of the media strove to give the opposite impression.

Australia's sea borders allow it, unlike the USA and even Britain, to select its immigrants. Hence the character and educational level of immigrants is not an issue in Australia. However the indefinite increase in population that high immigration might produce certainly is.

In this context the Australian Academy of Science stepped in. In a major public statement in 1994 it advocated ensuring that Australia's population did not pass 23 million, that sex-education and birth-control be encouraged ('every baby a wanted baby'), and that net immigration should stay in what it considered the responsible range. This meant below 50,000 a year (about a half of what it was in most of the Hawke–Keating period and about a quarter of the 190,000 to which the Howard government would push it by 2007, according to the Australian Bureau of Statistics). Aware that Hawke and Keating had traded on the public's tendency to confuse immigrants and refugees, the Academy pointed out that a much expanded refugee programme could fit comfortably within the 50,000 cap. Similar enquiries and reports by Labor's erudite Party president Barry Jones, and by CSIRO, came to much the same conclusion.

Instead the Labor Party worked out a way to update the old pioneering view that Australia was an empty country. Granted there was no spare farmland, Labor's spin-doctors removed reference to specific population outcomes and to what exactly all these extra people would do (apart from making our economy 'vibrant'). More importantly, it was now Australia's manifest destiny to build not so much a 'great' nation as a *diverse* one. Australia was to become a sort of one-country United Nations, in which a representative blend of the world's races and ethnicities would co-inhabit, miraculously unhomogenised yet on terms of the highest mutual respect, in a rich and democratic society. This was not a million miles from where Australia was already moving to; but as promoted by Australia's immigrationists it involved making Australia a permanent country of immigration, long after its colonial and pioneering periods should have been over. In effect, the case for preserving the continent's biological biodiversity was to be trumped by a new human-chauvinist emphasis on the 'obligation' to preserve human cultural and racial diversity: that is, to first import and then sustain these forms of human difference.

Thus, instead of being ashamed that we have lost so many of our marsupial species, many Australians on the Left seem more ashamed that we do not have a flourishing Inuit or Bantu community in their particular city. Quite why it should be Australia's duty to turn itself into a representative sample of the cultures of the earth is never explained. Instead, there are constant shouts that any reduction of immigration will lead to us tumbling back into an abyss of 'racism' and 'boring monoculturalism'.

Even more cunning was shown by the incoming conservative prime minister John Howard in 1996. Though one might doubt if Howard was even a sincere nationalist, Hawke and Keating had striven to present him as an ultra-nationalist 'racist'. Howard realised he could blind his critics by seeming to live up to this image. Each time his government pushed immigration still higher, he would monster a small group of asylum-seekers, or criticise an ethnic minority, and watch his critics lash themselves blind with moral indignation. Typical of the innumerate commentators was the *Canberra Times* journalist who scathingly dubbed Howard's Minister for Immigration, who had introduced the highest immigration in half a century, 'the Minister for No Immigration'. More astute was the *Melbourne Herald-Sun* journalist John Masanauskas, who noted that Howard had managed to double immigration while only being criticised for reducing it, and that though traffic, cost of land, and 'water, or lack of it' was on everyone's lips, 'yet a major contributing factor for all this is rarely mentioned, let alone properly discussed'. He also noted that there was as yet no sign of change from the incoming Rudd government.

Although Australia's population had been growing at a staggering 1.3 to 1.5 per cent a year, and half of it from natural increase, Howard's government ran a scare campaign about Australia's 'falling population' and even introduced a A$4,000 baby bonus – not to improve the care of the newborn, but specifically to bribe couples to have more babies. Biologists were not impressed. Recently one of them, Professor Barry Walters, demanded that, since the new Labor government has now signed Kyoto, the baby bonus be replaced by a A$40,000 'carbon tax' on all babies after the second.

The plight of Australia's cities, of home buyers, and of native species, all worsened notably on Howard's watch. Yet public opposition to current immigration policies dropped significantly because Howard never mentioned that he had doubled net immigration, and *talked* as if he were moving the other way. Many voters were confused by the baby bonus and assumed there must be a problem with population 'otherwise why would the government be shelling out to solve it?' – which may have been the point of the policy.

The commercial media were fully onside, and editorialised in favor of this 'wise' policy. (For them, doubling population in an area is like a farmer being able to double his or her area under crop). The Australian Broadcasting Commission (ABC) rather servilely followed the government's and business-leaders' line, though its investigative TV program *Four Corners* ran a 45-minute programme by Ticky Fullerton on how the Howard government had suppressed a recent CSIRO Report warning against population growth.

Most political journalists proved to be incapable of distinguishing between a falling population, a projected future downturn in population size, and a possible future downturn in the rate of increase of population growth. (Roughly the equivalent of a racing journalist not knowing the difference between distance, speed, and acceleration. The same tricks are regularly used in England and Scotland to raise concern about an imaginary fall in population.) Moralising commentators persistently confused immigrants with refugees. (Only a fraction of Australia's immigrants are refugees; rather, the emphasis is on cherry-picking the rich and skilled, and Australia is accused of poaching third-world doctors more selfishly than any other country.) Disinformation was also fed to overseas allies. Philippe Legrain's book *Immigrants: Your Country Needs Them* (Little Brown Book Group, UK, 2006), which was heavily promoted in Australia, contains a rich harvest of muddled statistics. These include the claim that Australia's population is 19 million, that its net immigration is only 90,000 a year (see p. 9), that births are not keeping pace with deaths (p. 108, in fact they are twice deaths), that immigration has been slashed by the Howard government (see p. 53), and so on. (A brief visit to www.population.org.au or to the Australian Bureau of Statistics website www.abs.gov.au could have saved him such errors.)

The real masters of the population game are revealed in a recent article by the sociologists Katharine Betts and Michael Gilding, 'The Growth Lobby and Australia's Immigration Policy'. This documents how a group of businessfolk (including developers and sellers of white-goods) set out to defeat the scientists' warnings against population growth. As their summary puts it, 'Immigration boosts Australia's population growth. A growth lobby concentrated among interests based in housing, land development and construction profits from this and actively lobbies for it.' They remark:

> The current [immigration] program is now large. But for some lobbyists the numbers will never be large enough. For example, in October 2006 Harry Triguboff, property developer and one of Australia's 10 richest people, called for a 'massive boost to immigration', aimed towards a population of 150 million by 2050. To this end, he argued that national parks should make way for housing saying: 'If people want to see trees, they can go to Katoomba, there are plenty of trees there.'
>
> ...
>
> Paul Keating labelled all NSW Planning Ministers the 'mayor for Triguboff'. Keating added that the 'wall of money coming at a minister is phenomenal because, as you know, the industry is into political donations *which in my opinion should be outlawed*'.

For Triguboff, Australia's economy 'is based on housing, which is based on a growing population'. 'Growth begets growth' and cities 'must grow or die'. Research by the Australian Greens Party revealed that from 1998–1999 to the present the NSW Labor Party has received $8.78 million from developers and the NSW Coalition parties (which are in opposition) $6.35 million.

The public record shows that growth lobbyists organised a pyramid structure to promote pro-immigration views, that they founded the Australian Population Institute, and that, at least in NSW, they gave large amounts of money to political parties. The interview data confirm that some of Australia's richest people are fervent supporters of immigration. The public record also shows that, no matter how high federal politicians push the numbers, some lobbyists will press for more. All of this may mean that, rather than having growth for growth's sake, Australia has growth for the growth lobby's sake.

As they imply, Triguboff is far from unusual in his class. (One remembers Philip Larkin's poem 'Going, going'.) In 2001 for instance Labor's Mayor of Brisbane, Jim Soorley, told the press Australia needed to triple its population in 20 years. What is saddest is not that such views are held by powerful citizens, but that the media, and especially the growth-obsessed Murdoch media, rarely permit any opposition or criticism. Ian Lowe, when asked why he 'never mentions population' in his public statements as President of the Australian Conservation Foundation, replied that he mentions it all the time, and the media selectively edit it out.

One reason Australia has never outgrown its pioneering and colonial obsession with 'filling the country with people' is that it shares the Anglo-Celtic property system which privileges private speculation in land. Vast fortunes have been made from this system by those who got sufficiently far ahead of the game to buy blocks of land, which they themselves did not need, on the edges of cities.

By contrast, the nation's capital, Canberra, was built on a French-style system, with the government resuming land from farmers at fair but moderate prices, auctioning it as cheaply as possible, and using the profit it couldn't help making to provide roads, schools, services and an elegantly planned layout. Canberra remains one of the world's most livable cities, and (for the developers who control much of Australia's politics) an embarrassing proof that there is a better way.

Most of the great fortunes in Australia (many of them, incidentally, won by people of Scots extraction) either have been made from, or have since been stored in and augmented via, real estate speculation. The recent Conservative treasurer Costello wanted the working class taught to multiply their money through shares and real estate, so they would not need pensions. Yet real estate gains are the ultimate form of Ponzi finance. The additional population you need to bring in, to buy up the houses of the existing population at prices sufficiently inflated to fund their retirements (in presumably some remote location where land is still cheap) means that the existing population come to have a much smaller share of the country they once owned. In Australian terms, such policies are a form of 'selling off the farm'.

Now, however, peak oil and the mooted demise of the private motorcar are questioning Canberra's pleasant suburban sprawl. Indeed, all over urban Australia there is confusion between those conservationists who are trying to preserve the suburbs from encroaching highrise and those more radical (or pessimistic) conservationists who believe that only much denser cities (plus public transport) will cope with future fuel shortages.

Some even doubt there will be fuel to grow the food for Australia's big cities, or to transport it there across the vast spaces that separate some of the state capitals. At least if the cities could be consolidated, some think, they could be treated as giant feeding lots to which the food could be transported. Others tout de-centralisation as the cure to future shortages; but they are spitting into the wind. Australians seem interested only in moving to the big cities. The country, especially the wheat country, is worked by vast machines and skeletal labor forces. Most rural Australians moved to the cities two or three generations ago, turning Australia into the most urbanised of the world's nations (other than city-states like Singapore).

One option that is fast disappearing is that of growing food in your own backyard, using the once-generous tap-water supplies. Rising populations, often dependent for their water on short coastal rivers, have begun to dry up the reservoirs. Politicians predictably have blamed the recent draconian water-restrictions on 'an unprecedented drought.' In fact what is unprecedented is not the low rainfall but the swollen populations now dependent on those dams and rivers. Federal and State governments have gone on pouring about a thousand new settlers a month into each of Melbourne, Sydney, and Brisbane.

Environmentalists have begun to discuss whether civil disobedience against water restrictions may be one way to bring home to some politicians that the age of endless growth is over. Meanwhile Australia's gardens have begun to wilt, and there is a thriving business in replacing lawns with xeriscapes. Yet just at the time of writing (December 2007) the planet has begun to flip from the El Niño to La Niña cycle, and rains have begun again on the east coast.

Early signs are that the incoming Labor government headed by Kevin Rudd is prepared to tackle greenhouse issues provided it can keep the economy booming. 'We were elected as economic conservatives, and we will govern as economic conservatives,' was one of his first public statements. His Environment Minister is Peter Garrett, a conservative conservationist who, when he chaired the Australian Conservation Foundation, earned the ire of poet (and doyenne of Australian conservationists) Judith Wright for refusing to speak out on population or against indefinite economic growth. In one tersely-worded missive she stated the figures and concluded tartly: 'Anyone who can't do the sums, stand up.'

Perhaps Australia is like a cruise liner whose captain is required to sail in the direction chosen by a deck-steward – whose priority is to keep the sun shining on the deckchairs in the saloon section, so that their occupants will order more drinks. In the words of NSW environmentalist Gordon Hocking

> Economic growth and population growth are the two main drivers of rising greenhouse gas emissions but neither is up for discussion or negotiation. As long as we stick with an economic system that needs to perpetually grow we will remain trapped on the road to ecological and climate disaster.

On balance, the evidence is, as yet, that Australia can't do its sums.

Endnotes

Re 'No rocky scene in England or Scotland can be compared with it.'
See http://www.lib.latrobe.edu.au/AHR/archive/Issue-September-2006/rolls.html

On Aboriginal foods and on 'bush tucker' see http://www.cse.csiro.au/research/nativefoods/index.htm and http://www.bushfood.net/bushtucker_full.htm

On the lost crops of the Incas, see http://www.nap.edu/openbook.php?isbn=030904264X . Also http://www.naturalhub.com/grow_fruit_type_tamarillo_relative_new_zealand.htm on the neglect and loss of many Solanum crops.

See Don Garden's very readable account of the changing fortunes of environment and environmentalists in Australia, at http://www.h-net.org/~environ/historiography/australia.html

On population-related issues in Australia see and www.population.org.au maintained by the group Sustainable Population Australia

On population pressure in Sydney see for instance
http://www.aussmc.org/State_of_the_Environment_2006.php
http://www.environment.gov.au/soe/2006/index.html

On enquiries into Australia's carrying capacity, see http://www.labshop.com.au/dougcocks/abernethyfinal.htm and http://www.cse.csiro.au/publications/2002/dilemmasdistilled.pdf plus http://www.science.org.au/media/pop2040.htm (re the Academy of Science's 1994 statement, published as Population 2040: Australia's Choice).

On the Four Corners report re Howard's attempt to suppress the CSIRO Report on 'Australia's Population Dilemmas' : see the transcript at http://www.abc.net.au/4corners/stories/s718523.htm and the report at http://www.cse.csiro.au/publications/2002/dilemmasdistilled.pdf

On misuse of terms like 'diversity' to trump environmentalist concerns, see http://www.thesocialcontract.com/artman2/publish/tsc0802/article_698.shtml and http://naf.org.au/stone.rtf

On the article: 'The growth lobby and Australia's immigration policy'
This was published in People and Place, but is available online at http://www.population.org.au/issues/Growth_lobby_and_immigration.pdf

On the public being confused by government disinformation about population stats, see ABC Radio National's recent Encounter program on population. Transcript at: http://www.abc.net.au/rn/encounter/stories/2007/2101209.htm#transcript

On French intolerance as opposed to Anglo-Celtic encouragement of land speculation, see Http://search.arrow.edu.au/articles/135692

Fiona Doyle

Extract from *Whispers of this Wik Woman*

What is Wik in the white man's sense of the word? My grandmother's people on her mother's side have had to enter the white man's law system to determine Native Title the white man's way. My people have had to talk to and work with anthropologists, solicitors, barristers and lawyers to establish some kind of agreement within the Queensland government's law system. Our people know our lore, systems and structure. However, the white man's system dominates and forces our Elders and leaders to step into the dominant culture to determine Native Title recognition and ownership.

The land, rivers, coastline, wildlife, trees and the land's produce all have distinctive significance to the original inhabitants of that particular area. When the white man comes in with his dreaming in the name of power, economics and financial gain, they violate our sense of belonging and identity. They interfere with an ageless, spiritual system, especially in regards to what country and produce of country mean to us as a Nation.

Is there room for co-existence between the two nations and, if so, how? Although the Wik people have this system etched deeply in their minds, hearts, spirit and psyche, it is also necessary that the non-Indigenous, dominant culture, as well as the law that determines how this country operates, recognises the Indigenous system.

Sometime in 1996, negotiations between all relevant parties in regards to determining Native Title in Wik country commenced. The process involved lengthy talks and a lot of travel, not only for members of the legal and anthropological teams visiting country to talk to people, but also for people leaving country to enter the buildings and law sanctuaries of the white man to present the ways and stories of our Nation. Back and forward people travelled. In December of 1996 my Aunty Gladys Tybingoompa made history when she proudly danced on the steps of the High Court after the handing down of its decision that pastoral leases and native title could co-exist.

'What time this business gonna end, girl?' was a question too commonly asked by a grandfather or grandmother during that time. 'We should finish this business now, we tired,' they would say.

These questions are the words of Elders that have now passed on. They died wondering if the fight was ever going to culminate in victory. They are not here with me today, but the memories of these strong identities will forever live in my mind. Their voices have become a foundational song that continues to feed my spirit.

Basically, the fight from our perspective is to establish recognition of why and how country is important to our identity and our existence.

Nana accompanied her families constantly to Cairns, Brisbane and Canberra. As an Elder, she had to fight. She had to meet face to face the white law men – 'long black dresses and Goldilocks wigs', as she put it. Or, as others commented, 'Why them mob wear them silly little wigs on their heads? They look like little children.' 'Because this one High Court now', another relative chipped in. 'They dress up them kind way when we talk big business. We all have to talk proper way now, for straighten im up.'

Nana would look the white man straight in the eye and say what she needed to say. Then she would shake his hand firmly, and say, 'I trust what you do will be fair, fair and right.' She would also often quote the Bible back to the white man. Her favourite scripture was taken from the book of Exodus in the Old Testament: 'You shall not steal'. She honestly believed the chances of being heard and understood would be high. Then she would use her own language to confirm her argument, whether it was her mother's dialect, Wik Ngathan, or her father's, Alngith/ Liningith or Wik Munkan, the language she grew up in.

Nana's involvement with Wik is not something she could have chosen to be involved in. It is not a conscious decision whether to be a part of it or not, and, as weary and time-consuming as it is, Nana, along with every other Wik person, would always be automatically involved. Even if Nana had refused to pursue her rights or the rights of the Wik Nation, it would not have been possible because she quite simply is already a part of the process.

The Wik people are a strong Nation. Certain persons can see into the realms not meant to be seen by the human eye. These people have, through various ceremonies, acquired the knowledge, powers and ability to step into and function in these realms. Song, spirit travel, imagination, sweat and blood are elements that make this kind of travel possible.

We, as children of this powerful nation of peoples, have received whispered warnings to tread carefully alongside the darker, more spiritual side that exists within our social framework. From my dual connection to both the Weipa and Aurukun side of country I possess a culturally-trained woman's view on all things pertaining to life. I am finding that all that I create as an artist, whether it be through painting, writing or dance and movement, depicts an expression that is a mixture from both sides of the Western Cape. This result is inevitable, as it is how I was reared by my family, both immediate and extended. Our people have functioned as scientists, healers, teachers, historians and artists throughout endless time. They did not carry a title, as mainstream society would. Certain families were and are still known for a specific skill or ability which, when required, is called upon by our community. A group of members from one family might be known as the singers during ceremonies, or as the dancers, carvers or artists, or as the Clever Men practising to both heal and destroy. Certain persons inherently adopt or are conceived with that specific ability or role within the community. I am a performer through and through. My white father would say to me in the short time I knew him, 'You didn't get it from me, girl. You got that need and ability to perform and express artistically straight from your mother's people.'

In early October 2000 an historic event occurred for the Wik People of Cape York, mainly the family groups who now reside at Aurukun, with a few scattered families among the surrounding communities. At this event, Justice Drummond declared that the Court now recognised Wik Native Title over our respective countries. This was a long-awaited victory for the people collectively, and there was relief that there would not have to be a long drawn out trial in court. I was fortunate to be at the hearing at which Justice Drummond made his ruling, along with my mother and grandmother. As I sat among the families, my heart saddened at the thought of our old people who had passed away. They died contributing to this fight and persevered in the hope that 'traditional title' over Wik country would be recognised by white law.

I was proud to see our very dignified-looking Elders sitting before Justice Drummond, and also the younger generation seated on the laps of their relatives or playing contentedly on the floor. His decision was made with the utmost respect for these people and the generations that will follow.

Outside the courthouse, the dancers celebrated the victory through song and dance. Each group performed dances that spanned hundreds of years, that ancestors had proudly passed down from generation to generation.

My sister and I held back tears and our throats ached as we watched Nana join the Wikwaya to perform 'Sara'. Angus Kerindun sang, which gave me hope that there would be no shortage of singers in the future. And it was moving to see Granny Norma Chevathun's girls dance as young and proud members of the new generation of Wik people. The other neighbouring Wik groups also performed their own dances proudly, as cameras and news reporters darted busily to and fro to capture this historic moment.

It was a very proud moment indeed. Part of the battle was over, but Nana had one more hurdle to jump. Where she would stand and how she would be recognised would greatly determine not only her own Alngith identity but also the identity of all of her descendants. Her Alngith title had to be recognised and recorded in this way.

This hurdle was in the signing of an historical agreement (Western Cape Communities Co-existence Agreement) between four Cape York communities – Napranum, Aurukun, Mapoon and Injinoo – and Comalco/Rio Tinto and the federal government, which took place on Wednesday 14 March 2001.

The fight to proclaim and maintain recognition of Nana's cultural identity as an Alngith woman came to a close on that day. It had been a long, hard, time-consuming battle. Nana appeared to be the only Alngith member of the Wikwaya clan fighting to maintain connections to the Weipa township end of country. In retrospect, I am left confused. The process leading up to that historic event was arduous and painful. If Nana was from a younger generation or even a middle-aged generation that was claiming something that could be challenged or disputed, then I could understand it. But the fact that it was an Elder of the Alngith that was being challenged in this way was beyond my understanding. That was what made it not only painful but downright audacious. Here was the only fluent Alngith speaker, obviously possessing a wealth of knowledge regarding all things traditional on both sides of the Embley River, being dictated to by lawyers, anthropologists, Cape York Land Council, certain community persons and various others disputing the fact that she had any title for the north side of the Embley River – that she had no right to be recognised as an Elder of the Alngith. Even certain countrymen, relatives, did not stand with her. They neither disputed nor supported.

We did not hear from them directly regarding this issue.

The pain that lay covering us, her descendants, like a thick heavy blanket is indescribable. My throat and heart ached. I felt a lot of shame in that last leg of the process. I didn't understand where the shame was coming from at that point. Was I ashamed of my grandmother or was I ashamed of her questioners? Where was this awful shame coming from?

I found in the last couple of weeks during the contentious consultations with the lawyers, anthropologists and the land council that I slowly began to avoid eye contact with Nana. I could not look at her. I did not want to look at her. Whenever I did, the emptiness she was obviously suppressing and the pain she was consumed by swallowed me in. If I did look at her I fell so deep, I found it such a struggle to climb back out of that dark pit of pain. How could they do this to her? I kept thinking.

I began to doubt my grandmother. 'Nana', I said one day. I cleared my throat and braced myself for what I knew was going to be downright cheeky of me. Her fingers cupped the sides of her favourite pannikin full of hot tea that I had just set before her.

She looked at me. Her eyes were sad. 'Arni?' she responded. 'What?'

'Nana, how come nobody believes you? Why are you going through this? How come nobody is helping you?

Maybe this mob is right?'

I was crumbling by this stage but I was in too deep.

There was no backtracking now. I continued, 'Maybe you got no right for this!'

Silence.

There, I said it! Nine years of holding her hand without a single shred of doubt and now I'd said it. I slowly came to question whether Nana had any rights after all. I actually embraced this notion for the first time. I felt sick! I was tired of this business. And if I was tired ... little old me being tired, then what the hell was Nana feeling? This black woman who was so clearly traditional, knowledgable, spiritual, intuitive, strong and instinctive, what was she feeling?

Nana just sat there, pannikin in her hand. She did not move, did not flinch. Not once. No anger. No reaction.

She just kept staring straight ahead. I think she must have been digesting what I had just said, mentally and emotionally studying those words her own grand-daughter had just let loose, the one she had prepared and taught all her life, turning around and questioning her own blood grandmother's legitimacy to traditional title and recognition.

She turned and looked straight at me and said what she had always proclaimed, 'This is my home. This is country for all of us. Old people bin tell me. Them fellas don't know. I know.'

And she continued to sip her tea.

A couple of days later I sat down with Mum and Lynette. 'Mama, Lyn,' I said. They looked at me. 'Youse think Nana got it wrong?' I had nothing to lose now.

Mum looked at me. 'Your grandmother knows who she is, Fay. Your grandmother knows what she's talking about. She sat with old people— Kepas, Aaron and Annie York. They would've told her otherwise. Look around at this mob. Look at them! They don't know nothing.

They're only blowing big wind for nothing, that's all.'

Lyn looked at me. My big sister, who was not always politically vocal, was now being forced to join the process.

'Faye, she's our nana. She's been teaching us all our lives.

Why are we gonna stop believing her now?' She said this so confidently.

That day I felt a closeness to Lynette that I'd rarely known. Lynette and I are very different in character and personality. Here was the one thing that bound us together – a strong, strong love and respect we both shared, for this woman, our grandmother, and the blood the three of us – Mum, Lyn and myself – had pumping through our veins.

A couple of days before the actual signing some representatives from the land council came to my house. They informed us that they had basically 'discovered' Yepenyi's name in the records listed as an Alngith man.

'Clowns!' I thought to myself. 'The hide of this mob!

That's what we've been saying all along. That's what Nana has been saying all these years. But no, it's gotta be written down by a white man before they'll take it into account.'

They left. Just like that! They never said sorry to Nana.

No formal letter of apology was ever sent to my grandmother for all the humiliation and pain she had been subjected to as a traditional Elder. It was like – Well, she can sign now.

We are still waiting for that letter of apology, even if it gets put on her coffin. We are still waiting for that apology to come.

Nana's identity, who she was, and who we knew she was, was portrayed and jigsawed differently by others.

Anthropologists, lawyers and other Aboriginal people were part of the group whose opinions my grandmother withstood. She withstood them in a dignified manner.

On that day, after much strife, she signed with dignity, strength of character and wholeness: Jean George, Awumpun, Alngith Elder, and Jean George, Awumpun, Alngith/Wikwaya Elder. She signed twice. Just as she has always proclaimed, she had a belonging, a connection, to both sides of the Embley River, as she had been taught by her Elders, her father and her people.

Even to this day, as I form these words into print, Nana still doesn't get recognition as an Alngith woman in this town. Oh, there have been several times, maybe twice, when she's been referred to as one of the oldest surviving Alngith descendants of the Old People. Our grandmother is not present to sit as a traditional Elder to open festivals or various events. Her name is not mentioned at speeches in recognition of her Alngith title. Nevertheless, the fact that our grandmother's signature is down on that piece of paper in the Agreement is enough for now. We had to see that through. As for public image, it doesn't really matter.

Our grandmother's voice and teachings are forever etched in our minds, our hearts and our spirits. We are Alngith descendants in our being and in our spirits, not just on paper. That's the difference between gammon and truth.

I could not sleep the night before the big 'Agreement' signing. It was an exhaustive lead-up to that historic day.

In one sense, I felt an intense feeling of belonging to the Cape, which filled me with great pride. On the other hand, I was apprehensive about the signing, for fear of witnessing my grandmother being dispossessed or ridiculed even further in public. I was afraid she might be humiliated and insulted in front of others, and have to endure even more than she had already. However, I held my head high, pushed down the pain and directed my spirit to prevail, for Nana's sake.

To see Nana finally sign in the way she did was overwhelming, yet it was still not complete. I mentally photographed moments that I had bottled secretly in my mind, never to be forgotten or overlooked in regards to my ancestry. Yet there was still a void.

I witnessed people, other people, telling her who she was and where she belonged according to what was written on paper by white historians and white anthropologists.

They also said that some of her own people, black people who were relatives, supported what was written down on paper. The only person who was arguing against what everyone else was saying was Nana. When I asked her why there was opposition regarding her claims of traditional country and boundaries, Nana would insist that people did not understand; they did not know or did not know enough. There always appeared to be a fine line between what Nana was saying and what the opposition was saying. Even the recorded history was to some degree supporting Nana's claims and at the same time contradicting them. Clearly, none of Nana's Wikwaya countrymen were there to explain to the Cape York Land Council her links to her father's land.

In that room that day, I realised that no matter how much my spirit was screaming, the people in front of us simply were unable to hear. They were incapable of understanding where this 76-year-old black woman was coming from. She was speaking from her heart, from her spirit, and the law was not going to recognise that.

It is written in the white man's records that Awumpun is indeed of the Alngith. The 'specialists' have interpreted anthropological documentation regarding the lands of the Alngith and Liningithl by a certain process, resulting in confinement of certain families to particular areas of country. In

Nana's case, Arniyum or Roberts Creek is anthropologically documented as Nana's main country.

Nana agrees that Arniyum is tribal place, but her argument is that it is not the only place. She identifies with all Alngith country as her country, not just Arniyum. Arniyum is one of several significant sacred sites.

When I questioned this with anthropologists their response was that it was not their interpretation of our traditional social structure that restricts and confines Nana to only Arniyum but our very own make-up of what was referred to as 'Clan Estates'. It is that concept that has confined Nana to being traditionally recognised only in country south of the Embley River as an Alngith leader rather than being recognised as an overall Alngith Elder of all Alngith country.

That day at the Cape York Land Council office, Awumpun was 'told' that her claim to the north of the river was 'secondary' and that her primary land was to the south. Awumpun argues that for Arniyum (Roberts) Creek to be her only place is simply ridiculous, as it is story place with O'olay Paanj Story there: 'No one can live in story place, that story place belong to all of us!'

In a nutshell, it is Nana's interpretation versus the specialists' interpretation of our own traditional structure. What they have done is they have applied the rules of boundaries in bright red and therefore 'cut up' the Alngith Peoples as a Nation. This has resulted in a recreated Alngith Group. This group has a new face, a face which we the descendants of Awumpun argue is not reflective of the true face of the original Alngith Peoples.

I am neither an anthropologist nor a lawyer, nor a historian, as mainstream society defines it. I am not qualified in any of those areas, but I do have a position that far surpasses all those qualifications. I am her grand-daughter. I am of her blood and I have a responsibility to tell her story the only way I know how – straight from the heart.

Jean George Awumpun – 'Nana'

Reviews

Hamish Henderson: A Biography. Volume 1: The Making of the Poet (1919–1953)
Timothy Neat. Polygon. ISBN 9781904598473. £25.00

Timothy Neat's two-volume biography of Hamish Henderson has been, as they say, eagerly awaited; and for Neat to do it in five years is, in itself, no mean feat. For Hamish Henderson kept nearly every piece of paper in his long and varied life and met, in his diversity of lives, so many people all with tales to tell.

A friend and fellow London student of mine in about 1952, the son of German Jewish refugees, on his first visit to Scotland encountered Hamish by chance in Sandy Bell's and was converted (for a while) to the cause of revolutionary, republican, Scottish nationalism. This led us in the student Labour movement down in London mistakenly to associate him with the stealing of the Stone and the making of the ballad, 'The Dean of Westminister he said to his men…' I went to hear Henderson, before ever meeting him, at a Fringe Saltire Society occasion in about 1980. He was to share the platform with a Gaelic singer. Ten minutes overdue, no Hamish; so I offered the New Town lady in the chair to go see if he was nearby in Sandy Bell's, preparing himself. She asked, 'What is Sandy Bell's?' It being whispered in her ear, she declined my well-meant offer. There are far better stories, but few missed out whoever met him.

The original press release from the Scottish Arts Council announcing its financial support of the biography quoted Timothy Neat:

> Hamish Henderson lived a life of epic scale, affirming and changing the character of his nation. He was a brilliant, many faceted man, but above all – a poet. 'Poetry', he believed, 'becomes people.'

So when I finished reading this long first volume and looked back for its origins, warning signs were there already. 'A brilliant, many faceted man' most certainly – and for nearly everyone a joy to be in his company; but to have 'changed the character of his nation' is hagiographic hyperbole that does his memory no favours. And that his poetry should reach 'the people' was an ambition unfulfilled, unless 'the people' were embodied as folksong singers and collectors and those present in the heady exuberance of old style far-Left ceilidhs for which Hamish both composed songs of the moment and sang so well. There are many versions of who are 'the people'.

The most worrying warning, however, with hindsight should be read as that the grant was for two volumes. There are some names well known to every general reader, but not necessarily known too precisely for all that they did. I think Hamish Henderson, George Orwell and Naomi Mitchison resonate like that. Jenni Calder and the four Orwell biographers would have all had enough material for two volumes, especially if they (I should say we) had quoted so much as Neat and at such length; but the general reader would not have been well served. So those who knew Hamish well will relish the scale of two big volumes, finding in the detail many surprises, big and small; but those wanting to known him well enough for the first time will be deterred both by detail and excessive claims. The career and character of the man are rare and fascinating enough without claiming that he reshaped national consciousness or was a truly great poet.

Neat deals well with the early years. Hamish was the illegitimate child of a First World War Scottish nurse. But was his father one James Scott, the black sheep of a wine merchant's family, as on his birth certificate, or one John Murray Stewart, the oldest son of the 7th Duke of Atholl, no less? Hamish in old age seemed unconcerned, or amused to play with both possibilities. Neat weighs these alternatives judiciously. The written evidence points to Scott, but so it would, he hints, if Scott had been bought as cover. When mother and child were frozen out of a censorious Highland village, the Spitall of Glenshee (which village and its lore remained deep and vivid in his memory), and his mother took a cook-housekeeper's post in Somerset, soon he was at a good local school with an exceptional teacher, and on to a scholarship at Dulwich College, where as a day-boy he lived in a well-funded orphanage after his mother's early death. And from Dulwich, onto Cambridge. None of these scholarships covered board as well as fees, so there must have been help from a real or surrogate father. Dulwich and Cambridge, about which he talked not at all to his friends and acquaintances, in Sandy Bell's or on the road, would seem an unlikely background to the bohemian activist 'sorning' or scrounging (for long the perpetual 'man who came to dinner') around the countryside; for it was everyman's duty to help him in the sacred task of red republicanism via folksong and ballads, both those he collected and those he composed. But at Dulwich and Cambridge he pushed himself forward precociously and pleasantly as the embodiment of Scotland. Neat actually says 'playing the Scottish card'. Those were the days when the English upper classes could be patronisingly sentimental about Scotland even if they didn't shoot there; not, as now, confused and irritated. His being a strident but willing stranger in a strange land perhaps went with his early and extraordinary facility for languages. Fluency, empathy, mimicry and conscious role-playing were all virtues of the man, more often than vices.

Come the war, these facilities and talents soon elevated him from the lowest of the low, a private in the Pioneer Corps, to a Captain in military intelligence in the 8th Army interrogating prisoners throughout the North African campaign and Italian campaigns, most of the time with the renowned 51st Highland Division. When they were withdrawn from Italy for the Second Front, 'returning to Britain without their "singer and philosopher" was an unfathomable blow,' says Neat. And he further suggests that Hamish was left behind in Italy because 'the authorities' feared that he could make the Highland Division a liberation army for post-war Scotland. Such reckless exaggeration is of a biographer who shares his friend's ambitions, paranoias and amiable fantasies too much to be at all objective. When after the war Hamish meets up with Brendan Behan's family: 'he quickly cemented an all-singing, no-holds-barred partnership that was to have a long term consequence not just for Scotland and Ireland but for England too'. Modern academic historians have missed all this. Neat can be careful enough with his facts (indeed sometimes he gets drowned in them) but he interprets them Hamishly. There was a trial of four nationalists in 1954 on corrupt evidence from a police agent provocateur. Hamish tries to organise a rally of his own to celebrate their release, and alongside him is Jeannie Robertson (his great discovery among authentic folk-singers). 'By every external measurement – a police head-count, an aerial photograph, an analysis of column inches – this rally in the Meadows was a complete and dismal failure, but as an act of witness it was timeless and sublime.' Needless to say Hamish's nationalism, like his biographer's, is indeed of that 'timeless and sublime' kind that no political party in the real world could possibly satisfy, whether old Communist or old – or new – SNP either. Nevertheless Hamish was the first translator of Gramsci's *Prison Notebooks,* which had such a great influence on the thinking of the New Left as the dominance of Soviet ideology declined. Perhaps it even gave us democratic socialists our last cause for hope in any fundamental transformation of society.

Just as this first volume is called 'The Making of a Poet', the second, promised for November 2008, is to be called 'The Making of the People'. Well, perhaps I should have suspended judgment. Timothy Neat is yet to make the case that Hamish did have a Maker's effect on the people; but I suspect that the argument will turn on a pretty partial or heroic definition as to who are the *true people,* those worthy to be people (or more likely an un-argued, implicit major assumption). However, judgment cannot reasonably be avoided in this volume on whether Neat should have said 'The Making of *a* Poet' rather than '*the* poet'. For he plainly ranks him as one of the great poets of our time. Few would deny that Henderson's *Elegies for the Dead in Cyrenaica* of 1949 is of lasting great stature, both in form and content. The Somerset Maugham Award for Poetry was a just and extraordinary tribute to a first real publication. Extracts at least should be in the major post-war anthologies or studies of modern poetry in English, as Neat rightly complains they are not, and nothing else of Hamish's. But again the friend as biographer goes over the top and risks incredulity about even the best firm claim. After a lapse of several centuries a poet must write about 'the whole world… not on one individual but on the collective.'

It was as a 'whole', and in the grandest company that Hamish wished his *Elegies* to stand. Who were the artists who embraced this 'whole world' in their creativity and philosophical vision? Hamish named them – Homer, Dante, Rabelais, Shakespeare, Michelangelo… and he knew that, however good or bad a poet he might be, like them, he was a man propelled by love.

Poets usually judge poets. I am only a keen if discriminate reader of poetry. But I think a consensus of opinion would be that the *Elegies* are the only truly great poems Hamish wrote. He was friends to MacDiarmid and to Sorley Maclean, and respected Norman MacCaig; but was he really of their stature as a poet? To make such a claim Neat quotes voluminously from unpublished as well as randomly published occasional *verse*, questionably poetry; and he regurgitates even far too much merry and polemic doggerel, brilliant for ceilidhs, army or tap-room singsongs and clamour. He mistakenly tries to unify by the teleology of 'the making of the poet' the diverse, talented and extraordinary life of a man who could engagingly present himself in different ways deeply and sincerely to different people in different circumstances. All of that has enough claim to fame and human interest to justify a major but a more tempered biography of a most extraordinary character.

Bernard Crick

Sorry
Gail Jones. Harvill Secker. ISBN 9781846550539 £12.99

Gail Jones's fourth novel, *Sorry*, invokes Australia's 'stolen generations', the thousands of Aboriginal and Torres Strait Islander children forcibly removed from their families until at least the 1960s, in the name of 'cultural assimilation'. This policy was the subject of an official enquiry in 1997. The following year, National Sorry Day was instituted. It was meant to 'connote the restoration of hope for indigenous people', according to Jones, who makes her position extremely clear.

In the acknowledgements she thanks 'Aboriginal Australians… traditional custodians of the land about which I write… This text is written in the hope that further native title grants will be offered in the spirit of reconciliation.' *Sorry* is an act of solidarity.

An academic as well as an author, Jones has a determinedly cerebral approach to her writing (or her 'texts'). Combined with her selfconscious political aim this could have made for clunky fiction, but she is too gifted a writer to fall into that trap. *Sorry* is an oblique exploration of an ugly chapter in Australia's history.

Set in Western Australia during the 1930s and 1940s, *Sorry* is narrated by Perdita, the daughter of an embittered anthropologist, who attempts to be 'useful in the governance of the natives'. Stella, her fragile mother, is obsessed with Shakespeare and named her after the 'lost' daughter of *The Winter's Tale*. Perdita is largely brought up by strangers. 'If it had not been for the Aboriginal women who raised me, I would never have known what it is to lie against a breast, to sense skin as a gift.'

Perdita's most stable points of reference are her two friends, Mary, a 'half-caste' teenager and Billy, a deaf mute boy. Mary is a child of the 'stolen generations'; she is sent to a convent, her despairing mother commits suicide. Mary's natural warmth (and the kindness of the 'Aboriginal women') is implicitly contrasted with the emotional iciness of Perdita's parents.

Violence simmers below the simulacra of family life and when the world explodes into bloodshed, with the start of another world war, the Keenes suffer their own microcosmic catastrophe, *'tyranny and release from tyranny, occur everywhere, and in every scale'*. Perdita's father is stabbed to death, Mary confesses, Stella declaims Macbeth and Perdita is left with a crippling stutter and a hole in her memory: 'What had lodged inside her? What had stuck in her mouth like muck, like vile disturbance?' It is in such physical terms that Jones explores how the body, quite literally, ingests suffering.

Although *Sorry* has elements of a 'traditional' novel structure, following Perdita from birth to adulthood, Jones is interested in how the experience of trauma can pinch and pull the flow of time. The murder scene, full of elisions and omissions, is woven through the chronological tale.

Perdita begins to regain her ability to speak with the help of Russian Dr Oblov, and by so doing, remembers the circumstances of her father's death. Meanwhile, Billy and his fiancée Pearl induct Perdita into the silent world of sign language: 'she had been barely expressive, when her stutter had maimed her and driven her to silence, and now she felt almost mystically extra-expressive.' The complex relationship between speech and silence is presented as poetically compelling, even a little subversive. When Perdita, Billy and Pearl visit Mary in the detention centre, they communicate using sign language: 'the secrecy of their meetings was troubling to the institution, but there were no rules, apparently, against speechless meetings.'

These themes exist in parallel with the novel's political aim. Perdita carries the metaphorical weight of the story as she begins to understand the true nature of her guilt, and the gross injustice of Mary's imprisonment. 'That was the point, Perdita would realise much later, at which, in humility, she should have said "sorry".' Jones perhaps overstates her case, but her characters are drawn with precision and eloquence. Left to speak for themselves, which they most often are, they present a poignant study of Australian race relations.

Jones is weakest when she overplays her literary allusions. Shakespeare strides like a colossus through the novel, flanked by Emily Dickinson and Daphne du Maurier, to name but two. Pouring so much of Britain's literary landscape onto the pages disrupts the flow of her otherwise fluid prose.

Although starting out as a tragedy – even a stylishly melodrama – which quickly deepens with metaphorical intensity, *Sorry*'s most successful aspect is its warmth, its promise of redemption through friendship and loyalty. With a lightness of touch, Jones evokes a tragic structure, borrowed from Shakespeare, only to release Perdita – and perhaps Australia too – from its scripted confines. 'I looked at the sky and saw only a blank. Soft curtains coming down, a whiteness, a peace.'

Hannah Adcock

Moving in Circles: Willa Muir's Writings
Aileen Christianson. Word Power Books. ISBN 9780954918552. £14.99

This first book-length study of Willa Muir brings together an account of Muir's life with detailed analyses of her writings, published and unpublished, public and private. One of Christianson's concerns in defining the nature of Muir's fiction is that of the relationship between literary modernism and Scottish renaissancism; another is the centrality of feminism to Muir's writing. Christianson's thoughtful and deeply researched study, which draws extensively on unpublished and archival materials, shows how significant a figure Muir is for our understandings of the place of the woman writer in the early and mid-twentieth century and of the nature of 'Scottish modernism'.

Muir, born Wilhelmina Anderson in Montrose in 1890, was the daughter of a draper and a dressmaker who had migrated from Shetland. Her intellectual gifts took her to Montrose Academy and from there to the University of St Andrews, from which she graduated in 1911 with first class honours in Classics. In 1918, while she was working as the vice-principal of a teacher training college, she met Edwin Muir, at that time a clerk in Glasgow whose keen literary ambitions had found an outlet in his contributions to A.R. Orage's journal *The New Age*. Willa and Edwin married in 1919 and set up home in London, working as teacher and clerk respectively, but becoming increasingly involved in literary circles and in writing literary journalism and criticism. In the early 1920s, they worked abroad, teaching and translating, in Prague, Germany, Italy and Austria, establishing a pattern of movement between Britain and Europe which persisted for many years. Translation from German texts, including the work of Franz Kafka and Hermann Broch, became their primary activity and source of income. The work of translation also stands as testimony to the Muirs' desire to open British culture to European voices and influences.

For Christianson, the work of Willa Muir also raises significant questions about the nature of the collaboration with Edwin Muir and the extent to which she – by her own account and that of others the better translator – has frequently been viewed as a literary figure secondary to that of her husband. Willa Muir's sense that she had subordinated her creative ambitions to those of Edwin Muir's comes across in a number of the journal entries and other personal writings quoted by Christianson. One of the challenges Christianson has had to meet is that of rendering Willa Muir as a figure distinct from Edwin, and to give a full sense of her independent achievements, in a context in which the two worked exceptionally closely together throughout their married life.

Some losses are entailed in Christianson's approach, particularly in relation to the cultural world occupied by the Muirs. We hear of Willa Muir's early studies in educational psychology and of the importance of psychoanalytic theories to the models of mind and behaviour represented in her fiction. We do not, however, learn of her responses to *The New Age*'s early discussions of psychoanalysis nor to the analysis undertaken by Edwin Muir with the Jungian analyst Maurice Nicoll, the account of which plays such a central role in Edwin Muir's autobiography. There is some extremely suggestive discussion of the part played by the vitalist philosophy of Henri Bergson in Willa Muir's most accomplished novel *Imagined Corners*, and of the ways in which Bergsonism is represented as a form of flux and motion – a 'moving in circles', indeed – which is opposed both to the rigidities of modern life, represented by a linear clock-time, and to the sharp outlines of modernist geometries. These insights might have been extended into a broader discussion of Bergson's influence on the *New Age* circle, and on London intellectual life in the early twentieth century more generally.

The gains in treating Willa Muir in and on her own terms do, however, outweigh any disadvantages. *Moving in Circles* opens up Willa Muir's fiction and short stories in highly informed and interesting ways, and delineates their central preoccupations: the stultifying effects of Scottish Calvinist culture on women's lives in particular; the workings and the results of cultural and psychological repression; the need for escape, in a context in which freedom most often meant Europe. She also gives a closely argued account of Willa Muir's non-fictional feminist writings. These included the pamphlet *Women: an Inquiry*, published by Leonard and Virginia Woolf at the Hogarth Press in 1925, which Christianson situates alongside the feminist pamphleteering of Winifred Holtby, Ray Strachey and Virginia Woolf herself, and *Mrs Grundy in Scotland*, part of 'The Voice of Scotland' series edited by Lewis Grassic Gibbon, in which Muir mounted a sharp attack on religious hypocrisy and patriarchal power. *Moving in Circles* also gives an excellent account of the autobiographical dimensions of Willa Muir's fiction, and of her memoir *Belonging* (1968), which Christianson discusses alongside Edwin Muir's autobiography: 'There is a clear contrast between Edwin's *An Autobiography* with its interest in the symbolism and allegory rather than the detail of his life and Muir's *Belonging*, grounded as it is in the details of their lives together as well as her interest in psychology and her own feminist perceptions of a patriarchal world.' Christianson's very welcome study paints a vivid picture of a powerful and highly gifted woman: it recognises work and achievements that have for too long been overlooked.

Laura Marcus

Mrs Woolf and the Servants: the Hidden Heart of Domestic Service
Alison Light. Fig Tree. ISBN 9780670867172. £20.00

Alison Light has written two books. The first, a socio-historical study of girls and women 'in service' in early twentieth century Britain; the second, a psychological study of the relationship between her servants and one woman employer – 'the rarest woman of our generation' wrote Margery Fry.

Light is a superb socio-cultural historian, both as eloquent, analytical commentator and as indefatigable detective.

> [Servants] were the first up, getting the family out of bed in the morning; they kept them warm, they guarded and chaperoned; they fed, washed and clothed the people they worked for. They scoured the grease and hairs from the bath... They were witnesses and eavesdroppers, allies and sometimes friends... [Servants] knew that their masters and mistresses sweated, leaked and bled; they knew who could pregnate and who could not get pregnant; they handled the lying-in and the laying-out... No wonder they were dubbed both the scum of the earth and its salt, as they handled the food and the chamber pots, returning dust to dust.

It is good to have that obscure and forgotten voluntary organisation M.A.B.Y.S. (Metropolitan Association for Befriending Young Servants), founded by Mrs Nassau Senior in 1875, here given its important due. (The forthcoming biography of Mrs Senior will explain why the Stephens, Ritchies and Anny Thackeray all supported M.A.B.Y.S. out of loving devotion to the memory of their friend.) But Alison Light's great discovery is the story of Lottie Hope and Edith Sichel's rural 'Baby Cots', full of her adopted little pauper girls from the East End, 1888–1914. Some 'rescue work' really deserved its name.

The study of Virginia Woolf's relationship with Sophie Farrell and Nellie Boxall is to me more problematic. I believe there really was a lifelong surrogate mother-child love between Sophy and Virginia. Quentin Bell has quoted Sophy's declaration of allegiance: 'I ought to be able to cut myself up among the lot of you, but it must be Miss Genia; she's such a harum scarum thing, she wouldn't know if they sold her. She don't know what she has on her plate.' What the multiply bereaved, suicidal sufferer from bi-polar disease needed in 1916 was a stable, reassuring, affectionate ally in the kitchen. But her cook for the next eighteen years, Nellie Boxall, orphaned at twelve, out at work from fourteen, was herself desperately needy, demanding reassurance and affection. She was felt to be intrusive, moody, bossy, manipulative – and loving the drama of a row. There *was* affection between writer and servant: Nellie's offering of seven pounds of picked blackberries, Virginia's offering of a cuddle and a pineapple, but there was also torment – on both sides. We gasp at the fury and spiteful contempt in some of Virginia Woolf's secret diary entries on Nellie but we also note that, as Hermione Lee says, 'She detested herself for [her] detestable emotions about Nellie.' She *dreaded* their recurrent showdowns. It would be going too far to ask 'Did Nellie Boxall help destroy Virginia Woolf?' but the writer was tortured by shame whenever Nellie succeeded in bringing her mistress's worst self into the light. No wonder she could not write another word about her after Nellie refused to shake hands at the final dismissal in 1934. The novelist was also afflicted by a class guilt that drove her to try to recreate the inner life of the poorest of the poor. But she knew she always failed and finally she cut the lavatory attendant from one of her last sketches, 'The Watering Place'.

Alison Light makes a huge effort to be fair. Nevertheless 'Mrs Woolf' is in the dock. And the mutinous feminist in me feels that it is not fair. Why does no-one ask who enabled Herr Rilke, M Matisse or Comrade Shostakovich to do their creative work? *They* could not be expected to cook and clean and serve as well as write and paint and compose. But, when not prostrated by illness, Virginia Woolf worked many hours every day of her life, reading, thinking, writing, re-writing, always haunted by the terror that she would be betraying all other women if she published something second rate in a world where 'The fact that women are inferior to men in intellectual power, [Desmond MacCarthy] says "stares him in the face"' ('The Intellectual Status of Women', *New Statesman*, 9 October, 1920). Each time she submitted a new novel she was close to killing herself.

Yes, it is right and necessary to recognize all that Sophie and Nellie – and Lottie and Annie and Mabel and Louie – contributed, for 'without all the domestic care and hard work which servants provided there would have been no art, no writing.' But we should not underestimate that other work, also unimaginably hard, involved in producing 'Mrs Woolf's' books.

Sybil Oldfield

Old Men in Love
Alasdair Gray. Bloomsbury. ISBN 9780747593539. £20.00

Old Men in Love is Alasdair Gray's first novel in fourteen years. When Gray published *Lanark: A Life in 4 Books* in 1981, he claimed that his first novel would also be his last, and he has been doing that more or less ever since. This time it looks like he means it. *Old Men in Love* is a big book, in which Gray rehearses the themes that have mattered throughout his career. But Gray the novelist has always been interested in the different ways of telling a story. Subtitled *John Tunnock's Posthumous Papers*, Gray's new novel is presented as a series of unfinished historical fictions by a recently deceased Glasgow pensioner, edited, along with his diaries, by Gray, 'a writer who lived locally and, with some success, had edited and published the papers of a Glasgow public health officer'.

Tunnock's diary begins with the elation felt by drinkers in Glasgow's Tennants Bar after watching the Twin Towers fall. He goes on to chronicle his attempts to write a masterpiece which, of course, is never completed. What we have instead is a trilogy of historical fictions, each at a different stage of completion. The novel is framed by sections from a narrative set in classical Athens which culminates in the trial of Socrates. The shortest story is set in Medici-era Florence and opens with Carmelite monk Fillipo Lippi and his assistant painting in a monastery. The third and by far the longest concerns a nineteenth-century evangelical awakening in the Church of England, recounted in part through the spiritual autobiography of the pastor at its centre.

As Sidney Workman tells us in the novel's epilogue, each of these narratives has its origins in one of Gray's plays. Workman made his first appearance in the epilogue to *Lanark*, which listed the texts that Gray had stolen from while his fictional critic attacked the author from the footnotes. Gray resurrects Workman in *Old Men in Love* in his most searing exercise in self-criticism so far. While Gray's baiting of critics has often had a playful swagger about it, there is something altogether more sombre about the mood in his latest exercise in meta-fictional trickery. We are told that *Old Men in Love* will be Gray's last novel, 'for he is seventy-two and in poor health'.

The challenge that Workman poses for Gray's readers is to read his book in such a way that it becomes more than the sum of its parts. This is made more difficult by the apparent lack of structural symmetry across the novel's different sections. The Florentine narrative seems abandoned at a very early stage, while the section on the nineteenth-century pastor Henry Prince could be a novella in its own right. The Socratic section in particular contains some very fine writing indeed. Early in the novel, Socrates' wife asks the famous philosopher what, exactly, he teaches the young men who follow him, to which he replies, 'I teach them not to be so sure of themselves.' This sense of uncertainty underpins *Old Men in Love* and it is key to understanding Gray's work from *Lanark* onwards. Gray's first novel was, to a large extent, about the failure of progressive politics in the post-war era. In *Old Men in Love*, this uncertainty extents to an even greater extent than before into the novel's narrative method. In Tunnock's 'Prologue to Historical Trilogy', he tells us: 'My own schooling had described history as a forward march from an age when low-browed cavemen killed their meat with stone clubs. To my own time when every sane British adult could vote for the government of their welfare state which had good health care and education and legal justice available to every citizen.'

Gray's insistence on multiple perspectives and ironic self-criticism, his refusal of narrative closure, can be linked to a loss of faith in history as progress towards the welfare-state socialism of post-war Britain, whose dismantling he has so frequently chronicled.

Alasdair Gray's response to political disappointment has been, simply, to keep writing. In doing so he has created a major body of work whose faith in imagination challenges its apparent pessimism. If *Old Men in Love* is to be Gray's last novel, it will stand alongside *Lanark*, *1982, Janine* and *Poor Things* for its insistence, despite the limitations in John Tunnock, that human beings can act in a world where freedom seems so limited.

Niall O'Gallagher

Shakespeare's Wife
Germaine Greer. Bloomsbury. ISBN 9780747590194. £20.00.

It's often said, unfairly, that the surviving evidence of William Shakespeare's life would barely fill the back of an envelope; attempting a biography of Shakespeare's wife risks, well some strenuous pushing of the envelope. Such a project demands considerable imaginative ambition and methodological resourcefulness and, at its best, Greer's study demonstrates how both these qualities can uncover the often fugitive traces of early modern lives.

Greer acknowledges at the outset that there are almost no surviving primary sources for a biography of Ann Hathaway, later Shakespeare. There is no record of her birth, her Christian name may have been Agnes – although this was virtually indistinguishable from Ann in the period – and she doubts whether even the information on her grave giving her age at 67 is accurate (it might be a slip for 61). Beyond this, there are only a few meagre ecclesiastical and legal records to demonstrate that Ann existed, most famously William Shakespeare's will with its disconcerting allocation of the 'second best bed' to his wife.

In one sense, this paucity of fact gives Greer an advantage. One of the book's strengths lies in its polemic against biographers of Shakespeare who either marginalise or traduce his wife, usually both. The elements of this narrative were established in the Victorian period: a boy of genius is seduced by a much older and designing woman and is entrapped into marriage. Fortunately, he makes his escape (eventually) to London and achieves immortal fame. This lazy account will be unsustainable after Greer's radical revision of its premises. Undeterred by the absence of facts concerning Ann Shakespeare's life, Greer recovers a far more persuasive context concerning the social, maternal and material experiences that she was likely to have had. Much of this is fascinating, with detailed accounts of the busy economic and social lives led by early modern women. Greer describes the social practices of courtship, marriage and motherhood that would have been familiar to Ann Shakespeare, the demands of forming and running a new household (perhaps including lodgers) often in the absence of her husband, the farming, brewing and baking Ann was likely to have undertaken and she even suggests the possibility of a business relationship with her brother-in-law Gilbert, a haberdasher, which proves to be a somewhat enigmatic occupation. Alongside this, there are equally compelling accounts of Elizabethan Stratford and its turbulent civic life: the Corporation struggled with the horrendous local landowner Edward Greville and represented, as well as managed, a community that was often stricken with famine, fire and plague. Ann Shakespeare emerges as a resilient, capable, hard-working woman in a complex and often demanding world.

Greer's central suggestion is that, in the absence of any evidence that Shakespeare supported his family as he established his carer in London, it was Ann who assumed responsibility for the household in Stratford. This is a supposition and it raises a perennial problem with the imaginative licence exercised in biographical studies, especially those concerned with poorly documented pre-modern lives. In this respect, Greer indulges in an exuberant amount of speculation and, more surprisingly, romantic fantasy. We discover that Ann loved her Will, termed unforgivably 'the Bard', the boy who taught her to read whilst watching the cows, and whose reaction to reading his shocking sonnets was 'to have tucked the little book deep inside the coffer where she kept her own possessions, opened her Bible and prayed for them both.' This doesn't seem to have worked as Ann later nursed 'the Bard' through his gruesome death from syphilis. Fortunately, there's absolutely no evidence for this so we can imagine a more tranquil end for Shakespeare. These are harmless, if elaborate, speculations but what grates is Greer's equally groundless and often acerbic dismissal of the scholarship of others. In a chapter where the failure of Susanna Shakespeare, Ann and William's daughter, to receive the sacrament, is explained as either due to her being a 'bad girl' or to her being in service outside Stratford – there's no evidence for either claim – and where Ann is identified as the 'original' for the shepherd's wife in *The Winter's Tale*, the far more plausible suggestions of other scholars are ridiculed. Generally, Greer's use of Shakespeare's works as a source for his life and that of others is cautious, however, and thus avoids the problems that beset biographies of Ann's husband. The book suffers from its own excesses and from the limitations of a biography derived from such scant evidence, but it's also fresh, resourceful and full of interesting material.

Dermot Cavanagh

India's Unending Journey
Mark Tully. Random House (Rider) ISBN 9781846040177 £14.99

Adhering to an unvarying personal quirk, I read the Acknowledgements section of this book only after I had finished the rest of it. Tully's easy yet measured conversational tone is there explained with his mention of the Teape Lectures in the section entitled 'the Starting of My Journey'. In 1999, Tully was invited to lecture at Cambridge, Oxford and Bristol on the Upanishads and the Catholic Church. The generous reception his lectures received gave him, 'the encouragement to go on reading and writing about the ideas' they have expressed.

Steadily travelling through different cities, countries, ideologies and economic realities, this book progresses towards a balance that Tully so diligently seeks. Begun under a mosquito net in Puri's BNR Hotel, the book ends in the holy city of Varanasi, which for Tully symbolises all that his adult years in India have taught him. 'For many Hindus, Varanasi is the archetypal sacred place, yet almost one third of its population is Muslim. It is Shiva's city, yet many gods are worshipped here and different religions practised. It is also the city where the Buddha said he would not concern himself with matters of ultimate reality, such as whether God exists or not.' Tully talks about the influence on his core philosophy of the Sanskrit expression *neti neti*, which to him implies that we should not go to extremes, that we should come to conclusions but we should not claim our definition to be absolute or final. This is succinctly summed up in his subtitle: *Finding Balance in a Time of Change*.

Resident in India, Tully talks about how he can almost physically sense the enormous pressure on the nation to conform to the Western, secular, materialist way of life. According to him, many among the influential elite in India cannot perceive a middle path, believing that you are either in favour of economic development and therefore of Western culture, or you are some antediluvian romantic. Most Indians will recognise here a cultural situation that is intensely familiar. With the same sense of delight one feels on discovering a new CD that has accompanying song lyrics, I greeted Tully's arguments and observations, comparing notes wherever possible. He describes himself brought up *as a Westerner*, but much influenced by India and notes that in *India's Unending Journey* Hinduism inevitably takes centre stage, exploring and exalting in the plurality that he believes Hinduism stands for. He devotes a chapter to his education at Marlborough and his juggle with the rationality drummed into him at school and his later involvement with the humility that he believes pluralism incorporates. Christianity is then proficiently reassessed in these terms as he tries to find remedies to the estrangement of British churches from British modern life by citing the example of the Catholic Church in India which, with its 'inculturalisation', demonstrates that Christianity can be as Indian as any other religion. On the other hand, he also delves into the stories of those in India who misinterpret this pluralism as a form of secularism established by Nehru, and of that phenomenon of those Hindus who talk about Hinduism without understanding the plurality of their religion. Tully projects the many sides that a story about India demands. There is a deep frankness and humility in his style that immediately establishes a personal communication with the reader and makes Tully yet another participant in a discussion that typifies the Indian's love for conversation. This discussion opens up to religion, politics, economics and sexual mores in the West. Tully believes that India is in danger of ignoring its own tradition and rushing headlong into adopting modern Western culture. He quotes *The Argumentative Indian*, in which Amartya Sen describes the tradition of questioning, discussion, dissent, scepticism and an interactive openness that Tully himself exemplifies and conveys so well about his subject.

He concludes, 'Throughout the book, I have argued that we should not fall into the error of assuming that the East has got it all right and the West has got it all wrong. For me, India acknowledges that we can never find absolute answers to the most important questions in life, but we must go on asking them.' The discussion is only just warming up.

Sria Chatterjee

Folly
Mike Stocks. Alma Books. Herla Publishing. ISBN 9781846880209. £8.99
Outswimming the Eruption
Allan Crosbie. The Rialto Books. ISBN 9780952744498. £8.50
Hawks and Doves
Alan Gillis. Gallery Books. ISBN 9781852354176. £8.99
Geography for the Lost
Kapka Kassabova. Bloodaxe Books. ISBN 9781852247652. £7.95

Was it a morbid masochism that caused Mike Stocks to write a collection – a *debut* collection – of sonnets, then title it *Folly*? Is that not baiting a critic? In fact, it is bait of a different kind, as once you've pounced at the obvious opportunity that such a title presents, you realise that *Folly* is a collection not only of technical proficiency, but of profound depth as well.

It is disingenuous to call this a debut: Stocks has already published, among other things, translations of the Roman poet Belli's sonnets. His facility with the form is therefore no great surprise. Where *Folly* stands out, though, is in its versatility, accomplished not solely in terms of the form itself, but in the thematic range encompassed by the collection. *Folly* is a portrait of our all-too-common shortcomings as a species and as individuals. Stocks displays an acute capability of narrating within the form, precisely placing the elements necessary to draw humour, suspense, or empathy from each short piece, and while it's true that some poems are carried off better than others, there are few, if any, that miss their marks.

Allan Crosbie treats similar material in *Outswimming the Eruption*. Unfortunately, Crosbie's poems are accompanied by a too-knowing sense of irony that stifles their potential. The collection begins with some promise, but its opening poem, 'The View from Jenners', works as a microcosm for the whole book when it gets mired in parenthesis and bucks its rhythm. Crosbie has a shrewd eye for hypocrisy, lending credence to his near-pervasive, ironic tone. However, he also tends to over-narrate, constantly undermining a poem's innate drama by spelling it out for the reader. This tendency seems to betray an insecurity in the presentation of his subject, and yet at other times Crosbie writes like a man in love, inserting personal asides or overwrought metaphors for the objects of his affections. All of this is the result of a reflexive consciousness passionate about its subject matter, and it serves the writer well in the instances where he deals directly with love, faith, and empathy. Too often, however, Allan Crosbie says too much, with little benefit to the reader.

As a sample of the tone of Alan Gillis's *Hawks and Doves*, take 'I don't know you, you don't know me'. This line begins the poem 'Blueprint for Survival', and if it sounds tinged with confrontation or merely an ambivalent resolve, then that's something of a start. Still, there is a complicated mentality at work in Gillis's poems, and it would behoove you to look deeper.

Hawks and Doves, as the dichotomous name might imply, refuses to accept one side or the other. It is a delicate position that's matched by Gillis's command of language. In 'Death by Preventable Poverty', the poem's narrator reels off the names of the flowers he's passing, while mentally reeling over the regularity of death in the developing world. Just as impressively and problematically, Gillis engages intimate relationships: 'Between us, I often wonder,/who's the spellbound nation, who's the Führer.' His choices of imagery and dynamic diction do justice to all the difficult ground the poet chooses to cover.

At a glance, it would be possible to call *Hawks and Doves* a work of cynicism. The poems venture that way on more than one occasion. However, Gillis's treatments are so multi-faceted it is too simple by far to say that there is true cynicism here. Instead I'd say the work is honest, even where honesty is not easy.

In the poem which gives name to her collection *Geography of the Lost*, Kapka Kassabova speaks of cities and countries that 'sleep//in peace without us. Yes, an insult. Never mind,/we're here. Uninvited, but we're here.' It is an observation that, for many, would befit the closing of a book. For Kassabova, though, this is only the beginning.

Kassabova's words are those of the young peripatetic – the poet herself has travelled widely – but while they carry a certain amount of the uncertainty that accompanies itinerancy, they ring with confidence and certitude. Her poems are inward-looking yet always perceptive, as well, of the material geographies, even where these are only 'cemeteries lush with centuries of flesh'. Yet here, as elsewhere, Kassabova captures the interplay of humanity and nature. Following this line (in 'We Are the Tenants') she points out that 'we have been nowhere forever./We are the ones possessed by arrival.'

Kassabova's work passes easily from the individual to the universal, and one can only assume that this is the source from which she derives such confidence. Though the book ends, this is a voice we are not done listening to, whose marks we want to go looking for on the walls of cities we've not yet visited.

Stephen Lackaye

Bodywork
Dilys Rose. Luath Press. ISBN 9781905222933. £8.99
Visibility: New and Selected Poems
Graham Mort. seren. ISBN 9781854114396. £9.99

Dilys Rose's latest collection, *Bodywork*, brings the human body before us in all its pathology and pathos, foibles and glory, attendant myth and legend. With economy, humour, formal mastery and lightness of touch, Rose subjects different parts of the body to the poet's microscope, often bringing character to life in a few strokes. In 'Obituary', the list of a prostitute's body parts succinctly suggests the banality and brutality of her work, while reminding us that the person remains ultimately herself and unknowable:

> her vagina was pay-as-you-go
> her womb was an empty nest
> ...
> her knees knew various forms of worship
> ...
> the love of her life is none of your business

'Weaver's Bottom' gives us the girl who is weaving the famous tapestry, 'La Dame à la Licorne', who dreams of marrying the tanner's lad, but suffers from bursitis. On the wrong side of the tapestry, '[a]ll Anja saw was a forest of loose ends.' Like 'Mad Hatter Syndrome', 'Esme's Toes' and 'Elsie's Phantom', this poem imagines histories of an underclass hitherto unwritten.

Rose has the fiction writer's gift of timing, planting seeds of meaning that will blossom later, informing what follows. 'Minerva', a prose-poem 'miniature' of a mediaeval historian who emerges as the far from buttoned up 'Pygmy Ice Queen' she appears, is a fine example of this. In 'Sailmaker's Palm', which won the McCash prize and is written in the Doric of the Buchan coast, the child says of the father,

> Fan he'd tak aff the palm, his haun wis saft
> n'pale as a scallop. A big man, plain as a sail,
> slow ti shift, but fan change blawed its gale
> aboot the hoose, he widna shy fi it.

Faced with the child's schoolwork, '*Nae use there,* he'd say'n stare at his hauns,/

his big pale hauns, beached on his knees.' Haunting the poem, at the end his hands are busy with 'seersucker/prented wi bluebells'n cornflooers' as he sews 'a new pair o breeks for his mitherless quine.' *Bodywork* is a lyrical, complex, marvellous collection.

*

> Today I'm shaving with a dead man's kit – your
>   father's razor salvaged from that Catholic council
>   estate house into rapprochement of a kind.

The way 'kit' and 'kind' suggest *kith and kin* is typical of the way Graham Mort's poetry can work subliminally on the ear to deepen its impact. In 'Shaving Soliloquy' the poet comes closer to the dead man than ever he was in life. And because the image of a man looking into a mirror underwrites the poem there is a sense of things being confronted. This poem is one of the new ones that compose the first section of the book (likewise named *Visibility*). Thereafter, the book jumps backwards in time, to include poems from Mort's earlier collections in chronological order.

    Mort has always been a master of technique, of 'show not tell', and his poems evoke the noises and smells of other countries, the unique atmosphere of other lives and times. In 'Flashbacks', time is cheated as we eavesdrop on lovers of the past and share their triumph, 'ramsons stinking on the boy's fingers//the girl's pleasure purring in her throat'. But the river stands in for time, always 'toiling to pull//the village to itself, stone by stone/from where their fathers lifted it.' There are several sensuous poems that immediately transport us to Africa, as in 'Bat Valley, Kampala', where

> The sky stammers bats: a host of sable tents,
> torrent of invert light; their flux of dark spews
> shadow on a dimming township's red dirt roads.

In 'Indigo', an attic bedroom in northern England and memories of indigo dye-pits in a 'blinding yard' in Nigeria come together in a bedspread's 'old scent of Africa'.

    Sometimes Mort's very fluency can get in the way of the poem, giving his writing a sense of being willed rather than felt, as in 'Drinking the Motorcycle', a celebration of technical language with the nuts and bolts showing, or

'Narcolepsy', a glittering tour-de-force, or 'Lost Voice' – 'Rumours of a voice began/.../still Cordelia-like, still/soft and low, still loyal to the king in me;' – a baroque joke of a poem, but feeling too heavy for its subject.

One of Graham Mort's most successful and moving poems is the triptych about his mother's death, 'Quietude', where his concerns of time passing, language, and memories of his mother merge seamlessly:

> a winter morning's hawthorn
>   berries she'd have loved
> ripening from the passing
>   tense I'm walking through.

Mort's judicious use of line-breaks brings an aching gravitas to this beautiful poem, whose third part, *Dyson,* blends humour and pathos, takes risks and triumphs over grief:

> I'm Dysoning the old
>   house
>   hoovering up
>   my mother
>   with this new verb
> ...
> Even her deafness seems
>   gathered here from worn
>   carpets and rugs into
>   a layered silence

Anna Crowe

Riddoch on the Outer Hebrides
Lesley Riddoch. Luath Press. ISBN 9781905222995. £12.99

There is something of a convention about modern travel writing, generally involving one or more of the following; improbable forms of transport, variously hilarious catastrophes and/or misunderstandings, and a lively but inevitably good-humoured exchange of points of view. The writer generally departs with satisfied curiosity and a new understanding of a different culture.

This is not such a book, but then Lesley Riddoch is not such a writer. It is true that she cycles the Outer Hebrides, from Castlebay on Barra to Port Ness on Lewis, meeting and interviewing many islanders along the way. Crucially, though, she starts from a position of a wide understanding of the issues facing these people who live at the very western edge of the United Kingdom; not least, continuing depopulation.

Among these issues, she discusses Gaelic-medium education, Sabbatarianism, the lack of affordable housing, and wind farms. There is of course an ongoing difficulty in that, while some accommodations with the 21st century may be necessary in order to sustain a traditional way of life, such accommodations may destroy what they seek to make possible. Ms Riddoch avoids being prescriptive in her solutions, although she does not miss the chance to air some criticisms of Scottish Natural Heritage.

There is certain unevenness in the writing, surprising in someone with Lesley Riddoch's experience and her impressive body of work, and there are passages which read as if they have been transcribed verbatim from a radio show. These passages give to parts of the text a certain informality which contrasts oddly with some very serious history writing indeed. Although it does freewheel from being a chatty travel journal to a serious piece of sociological discussion, this is a truly interesting book; for example, who knew there was a golf course on South Uist which was designed by the great Tom Morris? Or, the Bronze Age archaeology, which was found nearby, at Cladh Hallan, on further investigation, may be fantastically significant.

There are delightful and extremely helpful small map inserts to help trace the journey, and some fine scenic photographs, while chapter headings are illustrated with Gaelic proverb postcards. In 171 pages, excluding foreword, bibliography, and appendix, Lesley Riddoch raises some curiosity-piquing ideas which render this book well worth more than one reading.

Fiona Allen

A History of the Beanbag and Other Stories
Susan Midalia. University of Western Australia Press. ISBN 9780980296501.
£18.49

The title story of this collection – first book of Australian author Susan Midalia – serves as a reasonable measure of the other fifteen works included. Although 'A history of the beanbag' begins with a general introduction to this most alternative of seating choices, it ends as an intimate portrait of the lives of two women. It is not a history of all beanbags, but of a few very specific ones. It is in this specificity, this narrowness, that the collection fails, despite patches of artfully crafted prose. Midalia's stories take aim at some of life's most difficult moments, and at the ever-imperfect interactions which result from our attempt to deal with them and with each other; but many of the stories fall well short of the mark in terms of engaging the reader.

Although the writing is polished and the vocabulary impressive, the author struggles to evoke a sympathetic emotional response to her characters. The heavy reliance on first person perspective and an omniscient third focused exclusively on the protagonist both add to the sense of being on the outside looking in. Much of the emotion and struggle is couched in language which makes it superfluous to read in Midalia's biography that she has been an English teacher. And there is a distinct stiffness and formality – particularly in the dialogue: this is most evident in the language lover's paean, 'It's only words' – which had the undesired effect of alienating me from the characters and their various predicaments.

The perspective of most of the stories is predominantly and understandably feminine. However, I found the male supporting cast left a great deal to be desired – as boyfriends, lovers, fathers, sons, and people in general – and were, in general, a bit clichéd. From the wealthy monster in 'Cobbler, cobbler' (the narrator's grandfather) who was jealous not only of his beautiful first wife, but even of the hideous peasant plucked from her slave-like labour in his shoe factory to be his second – to the marginalised and demoralised father of two girls from 'Meteor Man' – a range of disappointing, disappointed and downright unpleasant men are presented to us.

There are exceptions, of course. In 'Such a shame', a young man sits in silent support of his aunt as she argues the minority view in a discussion on racism. But even here, why does the man stay silent? In perhaps the most positive presentation of a male in the book, a son is glorified in his mother's memory as she mourns his untimely death in 'Looking out to sea', but here there is the intimation that the son has committed suicide. In 'Halfway through the nightmare', we are given another quiet, supportive man who helps a woman deal with long-buried grief and in 'Put on your dancing shoes' we have a harmless, flirtatious septuagenarian who entices a bored, elderly wife away from her uninspiring husband. None of these males, though, stands out as a strong and positive character.

'Looking out to sea' represents one of Midalia's biggest risks, but is also the most engaging and successful story in this uneven group. Presented in first person, in isolated blocks of prose – disparate experiences and memories of a grieving mother – the relationship between mother and son is powerfully recreated. The story finishes by delicately assessing the merits of a passive suicide at sea, when in despairing parallel to her son's final hours, our narrator contemplates 'letting myself drift, looking up at the stars' in the night sea.

In contrast, Midalia's laboured story within a story, 'Cobbler, cobbler' feels awkwardly artificial despite its more conventional construction. The outright comparison of the story to a fairy-tale feels heavy-handed and unnecessary based on the stylistic conventions adopted. And despite the narrator's claims of their veracity, the fairy-tale caricatures of grandmother and grandfather are characters too stereotypical to be placed as they are at the emotional centre of the story. Particularly cringeworthy was the rhetorical query from the supposedly sympathetic mother regarding whether the grandfather might be 'the only man to have touched her, ever, with some kind of tenderness or desire'.

Midalia's courage in tackling issues such as abortion, suicide, sexual assault and domestic abuse must certainly be applauded. And the genuine endeavour she has shown in excavating and exposing the emotional experiences of her characters – along with the assiduous precision of her language – is an indicator of more positive things to come from this author. However, she has some considerable work to do to convince me of the emotional authenticity of her characters, and to make their experiences more relevant. Ultimately, I was left with the sense that the characters in *A History of the Beanbag* would speak much more powerfully if their voices were allowed to echo the imperfection so evident in their lives.

Andy Gloege

Catherine Carswell. A Biography
Jan Pilditch. John Donald. ISBN 9780859766852. £20.00

This is a chronological life, beginning with Carswell's upbringing in Glasgow and moving through her studies in Frankfurt Conservatory and at Glasgow University, her two marriages (the first traumatic, the second nurturing) and working life spent mainly in Glasgow and London, ending with her death in 1946. There is, unfortunately, no strong interpretative framework beyond the obvious one that Carswell was a woman writing in the early twentieth century, with all this implies.

Helen Cruickshank, in her 1976 *Octobiography*, described Carswell as 'a very charming feminine person, quick and witty… Honest and open… advanced for the times in her views of the relations of the sexes'. Reflecting family co operation, Pilditch's account is equally warm. Carswell's son and daughter-in-law actively assisted and her granddaughters contribute an engaging preface, celebrating Carswell as 'a determined independent woman.'

No really new light, though, is shed on Carswell's significance as a writer (ably explored in the 2001 *Opening the Doors*, edited by Carol Anderson). Sections on *The Life of Robert Burns* (1930), comments on the novels *Open the Door!* (1920) and *The Camomile* (1922) are, while workmanlike, lacking in detail. More usefully, attention is given to lesser-known pieces, particularly Carswell's vast journalistic output. The best parts are the quotations from Carswell's letters (her own and her literary A-list correspondents) and from *Lying Awake!* (1950), the 'unfinished autobiography' edited by John Carswell. The connection with Lawrence and his circle is fascinating, particularly in the light of Carswell's biography *The Savage Pilgrimage* (1932). Lawrence appears at his most revealing and personal here. During the First World War, for instance, he wrote to Carswell, in response to Ivy Litvinov's pregnancy – 'It is a mistake for Ivy to have children… they are a stumbling block now'. In 1918, however, he embroidered a 'little cotton frock in red and black-cross stitch' for Carswell's baby son. I would have liked more, though, about Carswell and her contemporary Scottish literary scene: MacDiarmid and the Muirs are only mentioned in passing (this despite the correspondence with MacDiarmid in Edinburgh University Library which, as John Manson drew to my attention to, Pilditch does not cite).

There is no doubt that Carswell deserves further and fuller attention. My response to Pilditch's book was to develop a desire to read Carswell's collected *Letters*. I hope this, in due course, will be possible.

Valentina Bold

A Vigorous Institution: the Living Legacy of Patrick Geddes
Ed. Walter Stephen. Luath Press. ISBN 1905222882. £12.99.

Architect Enric Miralles acknowledged that in conceiving the aesthetics of the Scottish Parliament building, Patrick Geddes was a major source of inspiration and this is expressed in every bamboo scaffold and ceiling leaf pattern, as well as in the setting of landscaped gardens and courtyards. Woven together by the binding thread of Geddesian values and projects, *A Vigorous Institution* brings together diverse reflections on his polymath interests.

Walter Stephen provides the sandwiching layers – an Introduction, and a final article on Geddes' intellectual liaisons with his hesitant disciple, Lewis Mumford, and with the American-Dutch historian Heinrik Van Loon, some of whose engagingly ironic cartoons on practical possibilities are incorporated.

The filling of this multi-decker feast is provided by a wide range of articles. Considering Geddes' deployment of innovative technology, Sofia Leonard discusses his use of dark glass slides for his planning survey of Edinburgh, while Anne-Michelle Slater looks at his role in the marine station at Cowie, where involvement of local fishermen with academics and students embodies the 'think global, act local' approach; a well-known phrase which was coined by Geddes himself.

Geddes' pioneering work in symbiosis and his holistic vision of a beautiful balance between the physical and the spiritual are the focus of Aubrey Manning's piece, which was originally the text for a speech delivered at the opening of the exhibition 'The Regeneration of Edinburgh by Patrick Geddes'. Rooted in place as he was, his spatial planning with its ideas of attacking poverty, disease, ignorance, idleness and squalor through town planning and 'conservative surgery,' anticipated the welfare state. James Mackinnon shows how Geddes did not believe in plans imposed from above, but in working with individuals and communities, thus developing 'local life, ' while retaining its 'regional character…[and] civic spirit'.

Mike Small follows the ghost trail of PG, the globetrotter, in Cyprus, Italy, Catalonia, India and Japan where the 'spirit' and 'consciousness of the place' find expression in 'responsive architecture'.

Stephen pays tribute to Anna Geddes's contribution in providing the bedrock of a home and financial stability through her housekeeping management skills, in what was, a 'marriage of true minds.'

Geddes would have loved the transcontinental epic journeys made by two environment-friendly projects masterminded by sculptor Kenny Munro, who provides an account of how the visions of Rabindranath Tagore and of Patrick Geddes were brought together in 'The Language of Rivers and Leaves' and the 'Song of the Rickshaw'.

Overall, the collection demonstrates that to this day the energies of Patrick Geddes continue to be transfused into vigorous institutions, ideas and projects that work *with* the environment rather than against it. His is indeed a living legacy.

Bashabi Fraser

Notes on Contributors

John Barker compiles indexes for books. His prison memoir *Bending the Bars* is published by Christie books: www.tvhastingschristiebooks.com

Will Brady studied literature and art and in 2004 co-founded a bookshop on the Greek island of Santorini. Having since relocated to Edinburgh and completed a postgraduate thesis on the American author Raymond Carver, he now works as a freelance writer, photographer and graphic designer.

James Charlton is the poetry editor of the Australian literary quarterly *Island*. His two collections of poetry are *Luminous Bodies* (Montpelier Press, 2001) and *So Much Light* (Pardalote Press, 2007).

Sarah Day has published five collections of poems. Her *New & Selected* (Arc, 2001) received a Poetry Book Society Special Commendation in the UK and was shortlisted for the NSW Premier Awards; *The Ship* (Brandl & Schlesinger, 2004) won several major awards. She teaches creative writing at pre-tertiary level and lives with her family in Tasmania.

Meaghan Delahunt was born in Melbourne, Australia and now lives in Scotland. *In the Blue House*, won the best first book category for the 2002 Commonwealth Writers Prize for South East Asia and South Pacific region and the Saltire First Book Award in Scotland. She is currently carrying out an Asialink residency at the Sarai multimedia centre in New Delhi and working on her second novel, *The Prayer Wheel*.

Fiona Doyle was raised in Weipa's Napranum community on Western Cape York Peninsula. She is a freelance theatre and dance performer. In 2003 she won the national David Unaipon Award for her entry, which was developed into *Whispers of this Wik Woman*. She recently moved to Brisbane with her three daughters and husband.

Ruby Langford Ginibi is a proud elder of the Bundjalung people. Her acclaimed first book, the autobiographical *Don't Take Your Love to Town,* was followed by *Real Deadly* (Angus & Robertson, 1992), *My Bundjalung People* (UQP, 1994), *Haunted by the Past* (Allen & Unwin, 1999) and *All My Mob* (UQP, 2007). In 2005, she received the NSW Ministry for the Arts Special Award and in 2006, the Australian Council for the Arts Writer's Emeritus Award.

Martin Harrison is a poet who has reviewed and written extensively about modern Australian poetry. Some of his essays are collected in *Who Wants to Create Australia?* (Halstead Press 2004). His *Wild Bees: New and Selected Poems* is due to appear this year (University of Western Australia Press; and, in the UK, Shearsman).

Pat Hutchings is Senior Principal Research Scientist, Australian Museum, Sydney. She has worked on coral reefs for many years in the Indo-Pacific. Pat obtained her BSc, PhD and DSc from England and migrated to Sydney in 1970 where she has worked since, and she is also a recognised expert in marine worms.

Gayle Kennedy is a member of the Wongaibon Clan of the Ngiyampaa speaking Nation of South West NSW. She has had stories published in newspapers and magazines and broadcast on radio, and was the Indigenous issues writer and researcher for Streetwize Comics from 1995 to 1998. In 2006, she won the David Unaipon Literary Award with her manuscript, *Me, Antman & Fleabag*.

John Kirk is a photographer based out of Melbourne. A former South Australian and Northern Territorian, John has a passion for travel and photography. He has photographed much of the vast continent of Australia and travelled extensively through Asia, North America and Southern Africa.

Karen Knight has written four collections of poetry. Her work has been widely published in Australia and overseas. Her forthcoming collection *From a Glass Kennel* won the 2007 Alec Bolton Award for an unpublished manuscript. In April 2007 she spent four weeks in Edinburgh as part of the Varuna Writer's Centre and UNESCO City of Literature Exchange Program.

Gordon Meade lives in St Monans, Fife. His most recent collection, *The Cleaner Fish* (reviewed in *Edinburgh Review* 119), was published in 2006 by Arrowhead Press who will also be publishing his next collection, *The Private Zoo*.

Les Murray has won many literary awards, including the Grace Leven Prize (1980 and 1990), the Petrarch Prize (1995), and the T.S. Eliot Award (1996). In 1999 he was awarded the Queens Gold Medal for Poetry on the recommendation of Ted Hughes.

Mark O'Connor has published sixteen books of verse, and is the editor of *Two Centuries of Australian Poetry* (Oxford University Press). His poetry often deals with bio-regions. Website: http://www.australianpoet.com/about.html

Tom Pow is a poet whose most recent collection is *Dear Alice – Narratives of Madness* (Salt Publishing). Three of his four full collections have won Scottish Arts Council Book Awards and in 2007 he received a Creative Scotland Award for a project on dying villages in Europe. He is a Senior Lecturer in Creative Writing and Storytelling at Glasgow University Crichton Campus in Dumfries.

Kim Scott is a Noongar man. His first novel, *True Country*, was published in 1993. His second novel, *Benang*, won the Western Australia Premiers' Literary Prize 1999, the Miles Franklin Award 2000 and the RAKA Kate Challis Award 2001. Kim's most recent book, *Kayang and Me* (2005), was written with Noongar Elder Hazel Brown, and is based on her oral history of their community.

Samuel Wagan Watson is the author of 4 award-winning collections of poetry, which can all be found in *Smoke Encrypted Whispers* published by University of Queensland Press.

Tara June Winch is of Wiradjuri, Afghan and English heritage. Her *Swallow the Air* won the Victorian Premier's Literary Award for Indigenous Writing and the David Unaipon Award. In 2007 she was named one of *Sydney Morning Herald*'s best young Australian novelists.